LOTUS ELAN
A RESTORATION GUIDE

By Gordon Lund

www.brooklands-books.com

Lotus Elan A Restoration Guide

Published by

BROOKLANDS BOOKS LTD.
P.O. BOX 146, COBHAM,
SURREY, KT11 1LG. UK
sales@brooklands-books.com

ISBN 1 85520 5963

A-LTENR

Printed and bound in China

ACKNOWLEDGEMENTS

It is on reflection that what I set out to achieve could not have been completed without encouragement from certain individuals. On approaching a number of publishers with my early renditions, synopsis and covering letters, mainstream concerns showed little, if no, interest in my work. John Dowdeswell of Brooklands Books came to my rescue and with knowledgeable advice on publishing matters of this type showed me the way. Many thanks John.

I am indebted to Alastair Florance of Lotus Cars Limited for permission to include drawings and information from their invaluable workshop manual and also to Autosport for allowing us to include the interesting Theo Page cut-away drawing on the title page. The book would not have been complete without the extra photographs of Jenny Stevens and David Bowers.

For checking the content and proof reading I have had great help from Phil Hoban who, as well as being a Lotus enthusiast, worked in publishing before his retirement. And Peter Waggett, a great friend from within the motor industry prior to his retirement and another Lotus enthusiast with an immense amount of knowledge.

Lastly to my wife, Johanna, who has shown considerable patience over the years with what can only be called a time consuming hobby. I would like to take this opportunity to dedicate this book to her.

Gordon Lund

INTRODUCTION

This book is intended for those people who like the look of a Lotus Elan and would love to own one. It contains information they will need before buying, and subsequent guidance for the restoration. It is written in an easily readable style, conveying the author's considerable experience in restoring a 1968 Regency Red Lotus Elan +2 more times than he cares to remember and a concours winning 1972 yellow over white Elan Sprint.

My Elan +2 (Rhubarb) just after its final restoration. The setting, Ullswater in the Lake District. 1992

The workshop manual does not always give the answer for those working with limited tools, often in a cramped environment. Where I have found a simpler way, I have included it. Against this backdrop, I hope to convey the whys, the wherefores and the avoidance of heartache when purchasing and restoring an Elan. If you want a blow by blow "how do I do this" scenario then read the Lotus bible, the official factory Workshop Manual. No owner should be without one. Also if you want complete Lotus history, original parts identification, comparisons between models, contemporary road tests and other colourful accounts then there are a host of publications on the bookshelves. They all make good reading, I have read most of them myself.

About the author
A family man and Chartered Engineer, whose mother told him that he had stripped his sister's pram when he was just four, with the poor lass still in it. The son of an engineer, his own eldest son is following in his footsteps.

Today's modern classics are what I grew up with and had to maintain as a means of getting from A to B. From early British motorcycles, each one now worth a small lottery win, to staid family saloons ranging from an Austin A30, Morris 1000s, Singer Gazelle, MG 1100, Mk 1, 2 and 3 Cortinas, Hillman Imps and the odd Escort for good measure. The only car that stood the test of time, creating the embryonic urge to drive something different, was the Mk2 Cortina, a stunning Aubergine colour, unspoilt, original 1600 E. This was purchased for £500 at four years old and then sold six years later for £1,000 plus the experience of driving a classic in it's own life time.

My Elan Sprint (Custard) on show in the main arena building at the Lotus Enthusiasts Car Show, Newark. Rally plaques and recently won concours trophy for the Best Car in Show at Hoghton Tower Classic Car Show, 2000

The Mk 3 came after and provided good, reliable family motoring, but what a bore. Grey porridge at its best. At this time our two elder sons, Greg and Robin, our youngest, Matthew, was not even thought of then, were becoming teenagers. Father began to think of two-seater, wind in the air type motoring. An MGB was top of the list, being the most popular, easy to maintain and run example at the time. On scouring the local press I happened upon a Lotus Elan +2 for sale. A friend of mine had had one in the mid-seventies that, I recollected, had two serviceable seats in the back for children. I went to see, and bought it.

The Authors Elans (Rhubarb and Custard)
Twenty years later I am still smitten by the Lotus bug, but am somewhat wiser. The Elan +2 has recently been sold after 19 years of intimate relationship. The often overdone expression knowing every nut and bolt in the car rang true with this vehicle, and on more than one occasion. Parting was like losing an old faithful, pedigree Labrador. It turned out to be one of the most reliable Elans around, because I rebuilt it, literally, all of it.

The +2 won trophies and clocked up the miles, indecently for a Lotus. 200,000 was the most reliable estimate, with a periodic stay of execution as necessary repairs and maintenance took place. The third chassis, galvanised of course, was replaced after the

Painting of Rhubarb and Custard depicted at Le Mans. A 34 x 28 inch framed action painting in oils by John Ketchell of Penwortham, Preston. The painting was commissioned by my wife, Johanna to commemorate our 25th wedding anniversary and my 50th birthday

restored un-galvanised Lotus replacement of uncertain lineage gave up the ghost after negotiating a French curb at 60mph. The engine had just succumbed to a third major rebuild necessitating a block re-sleeve. It was now a standard 1,558cc. It even

Rhubarb and Custard together. The Sprint engine had just been rebuilt

An early shot of my +2 in company of MGB enthusiasts, Brotherswater, Lake District 1984

became more reliable, probably because of the driver's even temperament and understanding of the car, that driven sensibly, these engines can cover extensive distances without burning valves or holing pistons.

At about this time, when offspring were gaining some independence, my wife, Johanna, announced that a further addition to the family was on the way. Lotus motoring seemed low in the order of things. As things turned out, the +2 stayed and a baby seat was engineered onto the central divide between the two-child safety harnesses in the rear. Imagine the scene at the Lotus Invasion of the Lakes weekend when two adults, two children, a baby and a Labrador dog extracted themselves from an Elan!

This +2 covered at least half a dozen trips into France, reconnoitred countless tulip-style tours across England and France, and was used on business trips to the far north of Scotland and the West

Country. It was a sad day when I succumbed to pressure from a business colleague that he would like to take the +2 off my hands. At this time I was well on the way to completing the rebuild of the Sprint and it seemed a handful to keep two on the road. Needless to say, a very good offer finalised the deal. I know the +2 has gone to a good home and we still keep in touch. He is under specific instruction that if he wished to part company with the +2, I have first option. Sharing the same garage, side by side, the two cars were nicknamed Rhubarb and Custard by my family.

The Sprint was an opportunist purchase as I only intended to buy some odds and ends for the +2 and yet came home with a basket case, ripe for restoration, complete Elan. Four years later it emerged like the ugly duckling into a concours-winning swan. I hope that it gives me half the enjoyment the +2 gave me. Time will tell.

Chapter 1

WHY AN ELAN

"Lots Of Trouble, Usually Serious" – Myth or Legend.

The Lotus virgin, an often-quoted term in Lotus Club circles, refers to people who have taken the plunge into the unknown, "Well it's only a car isn't it?" The mystique of the marque has all the hallmarks of prestige, uniqueness, charisma and most of all ELAN. The French definition of Elan is panache, speed, effervescence, style, liveliness, etc.

Most Lotus owners will give you a different reason for buying the particular model they drive. The legacy of Formula 1, the performance per pound (sterling), the road-holding potential and ride. You name it, the reason will be there. It is in fact all of these things and more.

Many buyers of old Lotus, whatever the model, will have come from motoring backgrounds where the very basics of automotive reliability are expected in the most decrepit of old bangers, given a little bit of on-going maintenance here and there. Not so with the Lotus. What you have to understand is that the Lotus, when bought new, was a rich man's toy. When passed on to second and third owners, after the guarantee had expired, the unfortunate owner then found he was on his own. In the mid-seventies, the cars began to suffer from neglect. Parts were expensive, if you could find them. Dealers were rare and scattered to the four winds. Unreliability became the password and the mud stuck. In the hands of unwary unfortunates who attempted to run these vehicles on a limited resource and experience,

disaster was the only outcome.

The rise of the Phoenix came from the enthusiasts, the specialist sportsmen and faithful dealers. The club enthusiasts who pitched grass roots knowledge with faith in the overall Chapman concepts.

From all this came a core of downright stunning restorations which ranked with the best and performed in historic racing and concours events to show the world that this car was really well ahead of its time.

It all came to a climax in the late eighties when classic car values took silly proportions based on unwarranted claims of financial institutions, media and the power of the Yen. The best Elans and many other Lotus found new homes overseas often at highly inflated prices. This in turn fuelled the market until the crash in the late eighties, early nineties when large sums were lost, particularly on exotica.

This left a recovering market that became appreciative of the fact that these previously considered fragile cars had something about them. Unreliability became the exception rather than the rule. People began to accept the cars for what they were. Sympathetic owners realised that driven expertly and wisely, the Elan could still show a clean pair of heels to comparatively modern machinery. Given a realistic, comprehensive maintenance programme and accepting its weaknesses as well as its strengths, the car could go on indefinitely.

Chapter 2

THE CAR - IT'S LINEAGE

Back street special to Supercar status

A legend in its own lifetime – enigma or hype. The Lotus Elan was a natural progression of what was a course of classic lateral thinking. Up until the mid-1950s, the accepted path to automobile performance was big is beautiful. In the austerity years just after the war,

Lotus 9 Sports race car. Lotus Enthusiasts Car Show. Newark. 2000

enthusiasts were making their mark in racing and tri-als with derivations of small family saloons. These set the stage to prove that good things come in small packages. The most famous exponent of the genre was, of course, Anthony Colin Bruce Chapman. His quick succession of mark/type developments indicat-ed that the man thought on his feet. His successes in motor racing proved this point for so long by his being one jump ahead of the competition most of the

time. Occasionally he made a blunder but then he who never made a mistake never did anything.

The stories surrounding the formative years at Lotus are many, and legendary, I do not intend to go into great depth here as there are many histories available. The birth of the Elan came out more of frustration than anything else. Chapman's fledgling company had achieved acclaim and success within a very short space of time. His attempts to bring the company into mainstream car production had nearly bankrupted him. The Climax Elite was way ahead of its time and would have been a headache for a large company to produce, never mind a small, under-funded concern like Lotus. Then again, the large companies would never have considered it in the first place.

Lotus stuck to their guns and evoked that great

Lotus XI. Donnington Lotus Show 2000

A very desirable Lotus 7. Coventry Climax power – ex Graham Hill car Lotus Enthusiasts Car Show. Newark. 2000

Lotus Mk 6. Lisa Rushforth at 3 Sisters race circuit, Wigan. Paul Matty's Sprint Championship round

instrument of success yet again. Lateral thinking was brought into play and out at the other end emerged the Elan. The basic design theories were all there as before. Lightweight, soft springs, stiff dampers, suspension and steering practices that affected the motoring industry for years to come. Engine power was not all that important as Chapman had proved that all-up weight and handling were the more deciding factors. The costly Climax unit was replaced with the now legendary Lotus/Ford Twin Cam. This far exceeded its early expectations and went on in its own right to fame and fortune.

Chapman had thoughts on a direct competitor to the MG Midget and went down countless design avenues in order to achieve that end. He still wanted to hold on to the concept of a GRP monocoque, like the Climax Elite, but could not achieve this through practi-

An early Lotus 7 at the North West Club Lotus Invasion of the Lakes

cal difficulties, costs and timescales. The breakthrough came in the concept of an origami, sheet-steel chassis configuration onto which was fastened the engine, transmission and running gear. This enabled the monocoque body to sit like a saddle on the chassis which, when all bolted together, made for a very stiff structure indeed.

The gorgeous, sexy body shape, some say cute and mischievous, enveloped a package that astounded the motoring press on the car's announcement in 1962. Its performance potential quickly came to light when the press got hold of it. They were elated to say the least. Eulogies were everywhere. Success in racing brought the car more fame, bit parts in TV and the movies brought the car to the public's attention, but only to feed the myth. There began to be something intangible to this little car. Something ethereal, so desirable yet unobtainable.

A Caterham 7, Chapman's legacy lives on

Steve Millward in action at 3 Sisters race circuit, Wigan
Paul Matty's Sprint Championship round

Lotus 23B. Paul Matty in action at 3 Sisters race circuit, Wigan.
Paul Matty's Sprint Championship round

Lotus Climax Elite road version. Proud owners, Steve and Jane Millward immediate right of the car. Perigord, France 2000

I love my Climax. So do we

My +2 shortly after I had bought it. The setting Ullswater 1982. Compare this shot with the one taken in 1992 (page 7). The trees have grown a bit

My Elan +2 and Roger Aughton's (NW Club Lotus Area Organiser) Europa S2 at Le Mans 1985

Times they are a changing –
Economics and Legislation

The demise of the Elan was almost as quick as its birth. Chapman's fertile imagination had again been in overdrive and the company's growth meant further developments. An urge to go up-market, and hence improve profit margins, had taken its course. By taking on the supercar competition head-on he produced outstanding cars of the day for what appeared to be bargain prices. In the light of these developments the Elan, its +2 derivative, and the Europa had to go.

The early cars were also proving to be a headache for American legislation, particularly crash impact testing. Both this and future emission requirements would have entailed such drastic redesign it was better to start of with a blank sheet of paper. The introduction of VAT in the early seventies also plugged the tax saving incentive on knocked-down kit assemblies of which many Elan owners took advantage. So the likes of the Elan and the other 1960s Lotus models will never be seen again in mainstream production. Other manufacturers have made attempts but have failed to reproduce that basic simplicity that is pure Lotus.

Rhubarb and Custard nestling up together. The Sprint's strip down had just started

Chapter 3

BASIC DESCRIPTION

Dispelling the myths

So what have we got here? A car that is as nimble as a Mini, would stay with an E-Type up to 100mph, could out corner virtually anything on the road, would out-perform all other cars in its class and return 30mpg under most conditions, even more if you could keep it off the carburettor main jets for cruising. It all sounds too good to be true, in fact it was and there was a down side. Because of the Elan's legendary performance, some early owners thought they were capable of much harder use; long stints at maximum revs and some owners removed the rev limiters out of the distributor in an attempt to enhance the performance in the gears. This had disastrous consequences, shortening engine life if not terminating it.

In order to achieve a marked increase in performance, the engines, and in fact the whole car,

Tony Thompson's Elan 26R. Historic races delight

required much further development. Enter the Type 26R, an Elan developed by Lotus specifically for racing, and even further by other concerns. These specialist cars showed up the basic weaknesses in the road going Elan, which vindicated the comments made by Chapman at the time that the Elan was never intended to be a racing car.

An Engineers Guide to the Universe

There is an old saying in engineering circles called "fitness for purpose". This enshrines all basic product legislation in what a consumer should expect from a product. No more and no less than what that product was originally designed and marketed for in fact. The Elan is not an easy one to pin down here, partly because of the claims of the Lotus PR department and what the customers of the day expected, against what the engineers who built the car knew what it was capable of. The Lotus PR and Sales Department had to do all they could to enhance sales. The image built up by the Formula One team was a big one to live up to but what an image! Of course advertising played up to the heritage of the road cars and the prospective owners expected no more and no less than that the cars should live up to this image.

Against all this pressure the Lotus engineers and service staff must have been gritting their teeth and waiting in anticipation for all the warranty claims. It must be emphasised that against this scenario, the

Elans in action at 3 Sisters race circuit, Wigan

Phil Hall's extremely fast Elan   *A Shapecraft Elan in action*

A +2 Elan in action   *EMA 359K on marshalling duties*

Sprints doing what they do best. Sprint

An Elan Sprint drop head coupe at
Donnington Lotus car show

warranty claims were not as bad as they could have been. Of course Lotus threw in plenty of disclaimers, such obvious ones as removing the rev limiter and other non-standard conversions would immediately invalidate any such warranty claims. For the most though, responsible drivers derived the best pleasures and healthier resale values than the less responsible. Because of its heritage, the Elan was a much stronger car than it looked, the running gear and motive power were extremely reliable if treated and serviced correctly. So as an engineer, I can appreciate that, in fact, these cars are in fact "fit for purpose". It all depends on what your purpose is.

Form follows Function

Another classic engineering design term, "form follows function" is derived principally from the world of nature. Why is a Greyhound the shape it is? How does a Swallow manoeuvre so nimbly through the air? Many other examples exist and are so obvious when you think about it. The lineage of the Elan has already been mentioned, and the virtues of light-weight and nimble suspension with sleek, aerodynamic body lines and lots of original thinking have produced a vehicle that extols these virtues. The form of the Elan is unique, others have tried to copy it with some degree of success but none have ever come close to the original concepts.

To the eyes of the general public, the Elan immediately catches the attention as an attractive shape that is serious about what it can do. To the enlightened owner, he knows what it will do and he knows why it is the size and shape it is. To an Elan owner "form follows function" perfectly.

The Progression of the Elan

The two-seater Elan went through four basic series with some degree of overlap at each stage. The Sprint model was a Series 4 car with performance and other enhancements added in order to boost sales figures.

The Series 1 car was introduced in 1962 but was not available to the public until 1963. This car was very basic compared to the models that followed. It was only available as a convertible with the later option of a detachable hardtop. The side windows were manually operated, sliding devices held up by counterbalance mechanisms and friction. They had no upper frames and sealed directly onto the hood. Carpeting took the form of rubber matting and the dashboard was an oiled teak veneer affair that did not extend over to the passenger side of the car. The door inner handles were folded sheet aluminium. If nothing else, the car was as light as it was ever going to be.

The first 20 or so cars were built with 1,500cc engines that were quickly recalled to be changed to the new 1,558cc capacity. Chapman had again taken advantage of a regulation that enabled Lotus to race in certain classes with engines above 1,500cc. Rumour also has it that he needed those 20 engines for other formula racing at the time.

Colin Chapman was rightly obsessed with all-up car weight and was at constant loggerheads with his own people to satisfy customer demands for additional refinements and creature comforts without incurring extra weight.

The Series 2 model followed shortly after with

The same car, rear end

The coveted badge

improvements brought about by further development and customer requests. The dashboard took on the appearance of a much more refined animal. Full-width, high-gloss, straight-grained veneer complete with passenger glove compartment. Carpets were added but with minimal soundproofing to save weight. Proper internal door handles appeared with padded upholstered internal door trim. Some mechanical changes took effect, such as larger front brake discs and higher differential gearing. Changes also occurred in the engine department to take advantage of some developments made at Ford, such as better crankshafts, connecting rods and sealing arrangements. Lotus made detailed changes to the cylinder head to incorporate additional stiffening, and the introduction of valve tappet sleeves in order to reduce wear in this area. The Series 1 and Series 2 were known as the Type 26, the last of the Series 2 cars being produced in 1966.

In 1965 the Series 3 car was introduced, which was basically a fixed head coupé made from an all-new mould. Body changes made at this time included a boot lid that extended over the rear of the car to help prevent water ingress to the boot, and also improve access. Door window frames appeared, with electric window winder operation. The rear light cluster was changed to a single unit instead of separate lamps. This car was known as the Type 36. A drop-head version was created in 1966 by cutting the roof off the bodies made from the Type 36 mould. This car was known as the Type 45.

New improvements came about in 1968 when the

Series 4 car was introduced. It still bore the same type numbers as for the Series 3 fixed- and drop-head coupé, namely the Type 36 and 45. Easily identifiable external differences were the flared wheel arches and new rear light clusters. Internally the dashboard went further upmarket with rocker switches replacing the old toggle switches. Detail changes took place to refine the interior and hood operation.

In 1971, the Elan Sprint was introduced in order to boost sales. This car was given a much-needed increase in engine performance to keep up with rivals who had responded to the threat of the Elan, hence the Big Valve engine. A misnomer as the only connection with a big valve was the enlargement of the inlet valve by one millimetre. But with judicious selection of appropriate camshafts, porting modifications, carburettor jetting and increase in compression ratio, a realistic 126bhp was achieved without affecting driveability and reliability.

It was available mainly in cigarette packet colours of red over white with a gold coloured stripe emblazoned with ELAN SPRINT down each side. The performance was electric at the time with a 0–60mph acceleration time of 6.7seconds. Top speed did not change much at all, and to the owners of the last five cars out of the factory a five-speed gear box was fitted. Colour schemes varied to include yellow, blue, green, pistachio, orange and a few others that I am certain where not in the book. Apparently at the latter stages of production a single colour car cost more than a two tone.

Chapter 4

WHERE TO START

Read Lotus Books

We are not talking rocket science, you do not need a degree in astro-physics or engineering to restore an Elan. Basic common sense, adequate resources, a lot of patience and technical know-how is all that is required. Common sense – you either have it or you do not, only you can answer that one. Adequate resources – we will cover this one later. Patience is not everyone's forte but can be learnt quickly when you realise the consequences of the lack of it. Technical know-how – this can be taught but only learned if the person being taught is receptive. The best way to learn is to read about your subject whilst you are doing it. You can see the point being made and quickly realise that without this information at hand the blunders that could be made would be costly in time, money and your patience.

A selection of books is available to give an insight into Elan restoration, some better than others. The most essential, of course, is the official Lotus Workshop Manual. Do not attempt to touch an Elan without reading this from cover to cover. Then read it again as you are doing the job in hand. The next publication is the official Lotus Parts Manual. This will give you some pretty good information and illustrations that do not always appear in the Workshop Manual. Other enlightened publications are at hand to assist you and it is recommended you read as many as you can. There is a list at the back of the book, certainly not exhaustive but I have read them all. Take what you can from them. Reading about your

A typical Club Lotus North West Area gathering

Concours winning Sprint, Invasion of the Lakes, Cumbria Grand Hotel, Grange over Sands

subject is only one way to feel confident in taking on a Lotus restoration. Talking to like-minded individuals is another and can be very rewarding as well as opening up a new circle of friends.

Join a Club

There are a number of Lotus Clubs for any prospective owner or enthusiast. They are in most of the leading auto journals, and they are all good value for money. Even if you do not take part in the club activities cheaper insurance, discounts on spares at some outlets, valuations and technical information are all available. Attending the club meetings will introduce you to the new friends mentioned before, but more particularly you can see first hand the fruits of their labours and pick their brains for advice. Many Lotus owners will be only too glad to pass on his or her experiences, some good, some bad. At least you will have talked to people who have done it. Not just talked about it, but done it. There is no substitute.

Befriend a Lotus enthusiast

This is a natural stage of development from the last subject. Sometimes you will become so despondent with whatever you are doing that you will consider throwing in the towel. A friend who knows what you are going through is essential at a time like this. Someone coming in fresh and pointing you in the right direction solves many a problem. If he is a good friend he might even help you.

Developing a Strategy – How to avoid Heartache

You have read the books, joined a club, made some friends, now what? The first instinct is to rush out and buy a car. Any car that is fit for undivided attention and loyalty for as long as it takes. BEWARE!! There are many pitfalls to be made that could impede progress or downright scupper the whole project.

Same car with winners plaque

Another concours winning Sprint, Invasion of the Lakes, The Ullswater Hotel, Glenridding

Plan Ahead

Ask the following questions. How long is it going to take? Think long and hard over this one. Many restorations have ended up as an unfinished project in the small ads. Add to the equation, how much time per week can be devoted to this without;

a) Upsetting your wife who will be as jealous of the time you spend in the garage as if you had a paramour on the side.

b) Neglecting your children to the point where they call the milkman daddy.

c) Your own dog biting you when you attempt to enter your own house.

The same car, different angle

When all these questions have been answered take the first answer, divide by the second then double it, at least. If the sums are suspect, quadruple the overall time first thought of. If this figure seems unrealistic, then forget the whole thing. Sell the books, let the club membership lapse, unless of course you have made some good friends who need a good co-driver, and put it all down to life's rich tapestry. If you are not surprised by the time to restore a car then you are either, well informed, or possess a well-balanced approach to reality. Either way you are on the right track.

In order to progress on any project, a set of deadlines and targets is needed. Set out a programme of activities that have to be done in order to succeed. It does not matter how sketchy it is at this time, fill in the blanks later. Do not just do it in your head, write it down. Putting down these activities on paper will give an insight into what has to be done and when. It will also be very useful in providing information for the last two activities, which are essential for the would-be restorer. Do not forget that targets are for aiming at. If missed, move it, simple.

Capabilities and Resources

Your own technical and practical limitations will predict how much of the work is done yourself and how much can be farmed out. This will also be partly dependent on how much money you wish to

Phil Gaskells Elan Sprint in the company of a new Elan and Climax Elite at a Lotus Lakes weekend

spend. Be realistic on this one. If unsure of any of this, seek advice.

Resources should include a well-lit garage with ample room to get round the car and sufficient storage space. A sturdy workbench with an engineers' vice is a necessity. A good stock of tools is a pre-requisite of any restoration project. If a good toolkit is available look at what else might be required. A good quality, $^{1}/_{2}$ in drive socket set is indispensable augmented with a $^{3}/_{8}$ in or $^{1}/_{4}$ in drive set. A set of combination ring and open-ended spanners will also be required. Good quality screwdrivers of straight and cross blade variety are necessary, and last but not least, a good torque wrench. The torque wrench is the secret of putting things together that will stay together.

Budget (As of April 2001)

Set the limit and try to stick to it. Remember that buying the car is the least of your concerns. You will know how much this will cost at the outset. The unknown factor is how much the parts, out-sourced services and other factors will cost. Lets start on the easy one. A Lotus Elan +2 will cost you anything from £2,000 to £9,000. £2,000 will buy a basket case or a very untidy runner in need of lots of work. £9,000 will buy you a very nice example indeed with all the bills and photos to show that all the work has been done.

For our purposes, as this is a restoration project, lets look at the bottom end. So £2,000 buys the car. If you want a two-seater Elan double this at least. If you want an Elan Sprint add on another £2,000. The car will more than likely have a "goosed" chassis. For the lowest purchase price of the car do not expect anything else. So in round money terms, that's £1,000 for the chassis. That will buy you a factory-galvanised replacement based on the original. If you want an alternative space-frame chassis with all the latest goodies on board, Spyder do a good combination to suit your pocket. The costs reflect on how far you want to go. For our purposes we shall stick to the original Lotus chassis.

Next there is the rest of the running gear. Suspen-

Phil Gaskells gorgeous drop head Sprint

Another shot of Phil's car

sion, steering, brakes will all need a major overhaul. New dampers all round with springs, all suspension arm bushes, and new front suspension arms if the old ones look badly deformed or corroded. The brakes will probably all require replacing with new, including the servo unit. A replacement steering rack will also probably be required.

Next the engine. A complete engine rebuild depending on specification will cost anything from £1,000 to £3,000 and whether you do it yourself or farm it out to a specialist.

Gearbox. Again depending on whether it's a 4- or 5-speed will cost between £100 and £500 reflecting on what has to be done and whether you do it yourself or not.

The body. This is going to be your biggest headache. What state is it in to begin with? This will depend entirely on the original purchase. If it is such a decrepit example it is often cheaper to buy a new body. The man hours required to repair or replace damaged sections, or rectification of delaminated matting due to ultra violet light degradation can be awesome. Let us steer away from this one. If you do it yourself allow £500, if you farm it out, allow £1,000 to £4,000 depending on what sort of job you want and who you take it to. Do not forget these days £1,000

will probably only buy you a cosmetic blow over which will look terrible in 12 months time.

Then there are all the bits and pieces. Do not underestimate the ancillaries. A new wiring loom £200, a new dashboard £100, headlight vacuum pods £80 each, new headlight units, new rear light assemblies and we have not even started on the interior!

For the best estimate that I can give, depending on how far you wish to take it, whether it be a respectable, reliable example or a concours winner allow £6,000 for a presentable +2 and £15,000 for a concours Sprint. This includes the original purchase price. Anything else goes in-between. Shock, horror, I hear you say, "I could buy one already done for that". Precisely. It all depends on how much of the work you do yourself. If you counted your own hourly rate for the project duration you would find that you could not afford yourself. The professional will do the work much faster. If you farmed out all of the work it would cost you three times the amounts I just estimated. Restoring an Elan is not cheap, but then buying a good one is not either. As I pointed out at the outset, choose a budget and stick to it.

Do not underestimate costs or any of the other factors I have just mentioned. The auto magazines are full of part-finished restoration projects for sale at rock bottom prices. Do not let yours be one of them.

Chapter 5

THE INITIAL PURCHASE

What to Look For

You will probably have an idea already on which Elan you prefer. If you want to carry children as well as adults then the Elan +2 will be your target. The same applies if you have a limited budget but want the Elan experience. Remember though that the saving will only be on the initial purchase. Most other costs will remain the same. Early +2s are usually cheaper than +2 S130s and 5-speed models.

Two-seater, or baby Elans as they are often now called, command a higher price because of their popularity and scarcity. Some have been written off, some have been exported overseas, mainly to Japan and the ones that remain are treasured possessions that people are loath to part with, even if the car is a wreck. So finding a restoration example is not going to be easy. There are cars out there for sale but the trick is finding one suitable for restoration at the right price.

The final choice may not be yours at all but finding something close that meets other criteria better. S1 and S2 Elans are rare and command high prices. S3s and S4 Elans are more prolific, the SE versions again commanding a premium. Further up market is the Elan Sprint and finally, drop-head versions of all models command higher values.

Avoidance of Dead Ducks

Steer clear of major accident and fire damaged examples. They may hold untold horror stories that will blow your budget at the first opportunity. For the same reasons do not attempt a much-modified car with spats, spoilers and wings. Do not buy the first car you see, you may kick yourself afterwards when you find a much better one, cheaper. Take your time and view as many as you can. Get a feel for what people are asking for their Elans. A word of advice to the unwary, beware half finished restoration projects unless you really know and trust the person you are dealing with. If you are confident in your own capabilities to assess the situation yourself or have access to expert advice then that is another matter.

Take a Friend

Always take a companion with you who is a little knowledgeable of these things. Someone who you can discuss the matters in hand. Who can also give a dispassionate viewpoint so that you do not get sucked in out of your own enthusiasm. Also two sets of eyes are better than one. He might see something you have missed be it good or bad.

Choice Criteria

Having narrowed down the permutations by now you should have a good idea of what you are looking for. Ideally, a car for restoration should be complete in its entirety. A sad looking example in need of TLC but un-messed about is the best option, but you may have to compromise a little. The benefit of a complete car is that it will give you a good basis on what the car should contain when finished. By making records of what goes where on dismantling will save hours of searching for information later. You will also find the

Look out for corrosion and cracking at the base of the front suspension. This can cause the turret to collapse inward causing front wheel problems

Colin Chapman's signature

bits missing from incomplete cars are the most difficult to source.

As mentioned earlier, the condition of the chassis is immaterial, the worse the better then this will be reflected in the price. Make sure though that any chassis damage has not damaged the body, such as catastrophic failure of the front suspension turrets. This will be self-evident by excessive negative camber on the front wheels. If they do not point straight upwards, find out why.

A car with a half-decent body and original interior is an ideal starting point. A bonus would be an original steering wheel with Colin Chapman's signature on it as well. These are hard to locate. If you can find one, they command a very high price.

A car without an engine or transmission is also an unlikely contender unless you just happen to have a spare twin cam in the garden shed waiting for a good home. Current asking prices for complete twin cam engines in assorted conditions seen at various classic car shows will make your hair curl.

Where to Buy

You now know precisely what you are looking for. Where do you find this proverbial needle in a

haystack? Unless you are extremely lucky it is not going to be close to where you live. So plan a strategy as thorough as all the previous work you have done up to this stage. Scour all the periodicals and magazines as much as possible. Use the Internet. Make a list of all possible contenders who are looking for your money.

There is very little difference between trade and private sales in the whole scheme of things. The Lotus specialists may be able to help you in finding a car to suit your requirements, but you will end up paying a little over the odds. It may be the easier route to take in the long run as the specialist will see in you a new customer for parts and may help you along the way. Building a friendly relationship with specialists does have its good points. He may even sell you parts at discounted prices if you are lucky. One thing you will not get and that is any form of guarantee. What you see is what you get. Nothing more, nothing less. If you are having the car delivered, make a careful note of everything on the car and any loose bits that may be inside as part of the deal just in case any parts get lost in transit.

Buying privately can be rewarding but time consuming and may involve a lot of travel. This is when your list of prospective purchases comes in handy. If you have a good list of cars that meet your requirements, obtain names, addresses and phone numbers.

Camshaft chain tension screw. If this is well in, a new chain will be required

Keep to the closest one first and ring round and make sure the car is still for sale. Confirm that it is the car as described in the advert, then make an appointment to view. View as many as you can within a short space of time. If nothing appears suitable, then go further afield. You may end up going back to one you viewed earlier, but at least convince yourself that you have seen as many as possible before making a discerning decision.

The Sale

You have found the car that best suits your purposes. Now you have to make it yours. If you are buying from a dealer, take cognisance of the earlier comments. All dealers will barter to a point, but remember, he has had more practice than you have. Do not expect a great reduction on what he is asking. He knows the market and he will be prepared to wait for someone else who will pay his price. What he will probably barter on is spare parts that he will know you need immediately, a new chassis for instance.

The private vendor will be more amenable to barter. He knows that a dealer will give him only a rock bottom price and he will be hoping to improve on that.

Do not be too eager to make an offer. Give the car a thorough inspection and note all its misgivings. It will have plenty. Do not antagonise the vendor but be realistic and make what you consider to be a fair offer, having first established what his bottom price would be. If he is asking what you consider to be silly money and he will not budge, walk away leaving your phone number. Go and look at some thing else. If nothing else turns up he may ring you back when he has had time to think.

Before parting with your hard earned cash, make sure that the car is the vendor's to sell. An HPI check is useful here since it may also contain details of the vehicles history, e.g. number of owners, original registration number, insurance claims, etc., in addition to any outstanding commitment to a bank or other financial institution.

If you are fortunate, the future car of your dreams is now in your drive. You are full of aspirations, your wife will shrug her shoulders, your kids will think you have gone mad and the neighbours will be taking bets that it will never see the light of day.

Chapter 6

BITE THE BULLET - REFLECT
GET STUCK IN

Assess the Situation

Now you have the time to look at what you have bought in the cold light of day. Take your time. The old adage "Rome wasn't built in a day" never rang so true. You have done your homework. You know what has to be done. Do not, I repeat, do not start pulling the car apart straight away. Think long and hard about it and in what order it should be done.

The Importance of Photography

Obtain plenty of film for your camera. Then get snapping. Take pictures of the car from every angle, inside and out. Remove the bonnet, take every conceivable angle, where you can get a good view in good light, of every component that will be removed. Use flash if you have to.

Many people will make the mistake of removing parts from a car, convinced that they will remember where it came from. Wrong! This tip is the best advice I can give to anyone. It will be obvious also from this statement that photographs taken at every stage of the restoration will be useful, the build stage in particular. These photographs will be worth more than any stack of bills that you collect throughout the whole project. If at any time you have to sell the car, they will be worth their weight in gold.

Take Notes

Again, for the same reasons as the photographs, copious notes will serve as a useful reference at a later date. A logbook is the best thing or even a large diary. Make a note of everything you do. Record dates, items bought and for how much. Set up a loose-leaf file or folder where key information, bills, records, measurements and readings can be kept. Historic records like these will add to your own satisfaction and will count for a lot if you ever sell the car.

Organisation is the Key

A long-term restoration project can lead to all kinds of frustrations. The worst is not being able to find things when you want them. First, but not least, keep your tools clean and tidy. If you have not got a good tool box, get one. If you have a tool rack on the garage wall, use it. Spanners loaded with grease and grit will do more harm than good. Keep the workbench clean and tidy at all times and clean up any oil spillage immediately. Keep the garage floor clean and tidy and sweep it out regularly.

Create storage space, you are going to need it. Use plenty of good cardboard, or better still plastic, storage boxes. Obtain plastic bags of all sizes to put things into so items do not get damaged, covered in grit, or worst of all corroded whilst in storage. Label everything so you can identify where it came from later. Mark items left or right hand side, it is so easy to mix things up if you are not careful.

Set the Stage

Now you have a clean and organised garage, keep it that way. Give the family orders to the same effect and any bikes, scooters and bags of household rub-

Note carpets on garage floor and plenty of storage cabinets, table and boxes

bish are stored under the strictest of regulations. Kept tidy it will encourage others to do the same. Take it from me you will have a running battle on your hands, unless your garage is at the other end of town.

A further tip for your own comfort, get hold of as much old carpet as you can and lay it on the garage floor around the car. Nylon carpet squares are the best if you can acquire them cheaply, they can be moved around as required and are relatively easy to clean. It will keep you warm in winter and is much better than lying on concrete.

Chapter 7

THE STRIP DOWN

Safety Precautions

Fire in a garage is one of your greatest perils. All the ingredients for a massive conflagration are present, such as petrol, cleaning fluids, lubricants, paint, thinners, welding equipment, battery chargers and so on. If you smoke, stay outside. A Lotus of any description makes for a good bonfire, toasted shredded wheat springs to mind. Once alight they will burn with great fury. The essence of this little tale is have a good fire extinguisher, fully charged and ready at all times. Make sure you know how to use it before you need it.

Static objects never killed anyone, unless you run into them. Heavy objects will do serious damage to you if they fall on you. Many a DIY car mechanic has been maimed if not killed by a car falling on them. Never work under a car unless it is well chocked up on axle stands or better still, on off cuts of railway sleepers. Working under a car held up only by a jack of any description is stupid. Take it from me, it is not worth the risk.

Remove the battery from the car and store fully charged away from frost. Drain the fuel tank, storing the petrol in suitably marked cans, which can be used for cleaning later.

Preparation

The best place to start any strip down is to take out the seats and all carpeting. Store them in the attic, covered in plastic bin bags to keep out dust and spi-ders. This will ease the storage space problems in the garage and keep them out of the damp. If you have the room in the garage to store the body next to or behind the chassis, take out the front and rear screens. If the body has to be stored out doors, keep them in the car. If room is tight then use the body interior as temporary storage space.

Engine Ancillaries

Starting in the engine bay, drain and remove the radiator, air intake pipe, air box and carburettors, disconnecting all control cables first. Disconnect the heater pipes and all electrical connections to the engine, not forgetting the reversing light connections on the gearbox. Disconnect the vacuum pipe connections at the cylinder head. Raise the rear of the car, support on stands and remove the silencer and intermediate exhaust pipe. On the baby Elan, unbolt the exhaust side engine mount from the chassis and raise the engine on a jack, sufficient to unscrew the heater control valve from the cylinder head. Reconnect the engine mount back to the chassis.

Lighten the Load

Take as much weight out of the car as you can by removing everything as much as possible. Take out the centre console, the door trims, window winder motors and door window frames complete with glass.

Removal and Disconnection of body to chassis Components

Unbolt the steering joint at the rack and column and

Plus 2 body placed on railway sleepers

disconnect it from brackets under the dashboard. Remove the steering column complete with steering wheel. Disconnect the hydraulic pipes to master cylinders. Disconnect the petrol feed pipe at the tank and the petrol pump on the engine. On the +2, disconnect the brake light wiring on the chassis mounted switch close to the oil filter. Remove all cunningly hidden earth straps from body components to the chassis, the radio aerial is favourite, sometimes connected to one of the differential top mountings.

Disconnection of Body to Chassis

Following the workshop manual to the letter, which I hope you have been doing already, remove all body to chassis bolts and nuts. The next procedure is to round up as many able bodied males as you can find, eight for a +2, six for a two-seater, including yourself. Two people to guide and direct, including yourself, is recommended, the remaining reluctant volunteers do the lifting.

The Lift

Never lift an Elan at the nose or the tail or even at the wings. Damage is bound to occur. Lift at the sills and as close to the edges of the wings as possible. Jiggle the body around a bit and release the inherent stiction that always occurs after years of being mated to a rusty old chassis. At this stage you may find that you have forgotten the inner seat belt mountings, or you will notice something preventing the body from separating from the chassis. You have either missed a chassis-mounting bolt, read the manual again, and/or some past owner has bolted on a non-standard bit just to confuse you. Either way, care and patience is the key, if you want to prevent unnecessary damage.

Having decided where the body is to reside for the duration, position the recently obtained off cuts of railway sleepers, one for each corner. Lift off the body and place on sleepers. Easy isn't it? You will have noticed by now that we have not removed the engine. Did you remember to remove the back two carburettor studs? The engine is much easier to work on and remove with the body off. Take my word for it.

Chapter 8

BODY RESTORATION

DIY Body Work

There are no short cuts, no magic words or whatever. It takes a professional 200 man-hours on average to prepare a fibreglass body fit to receive a topcoat. It takes 20 minutes to apply the paint. If you are determined to do this yourself and you have the kit and the knowledge, then go to it. Seriously though, there is a lot of satisfaction to be gained in preparing and

My Sprint in early restoration days.
The new chassis awaits

spraying the car yourself, if you have the where-with-all to do it.

If you have separate premises for preparation, a dust-free, temperature and moisture controlled heated spray booth and professional spraying equipment complete with compressor, you could produce a concours paint job. For the rest of us though, plan your bodywork for the warmer, dryer part of the year. Work in a well-ventilated area and keep dust to a minimum when you are applying paint. Be sure to follow the paint manufacturers COSHH details that will outline the safety hazards and what measures to have in place to alleviate those hazards. This is most important as some paint products contain very hazardous materials. Reading books on working on GRP bodies is strongly recommended as there are a lot of pitfalls for the uninitiated to fall into. You only want to do the job once.

My Sprint in early restoration days.
The new chassis awaits

Hard at it

Under tray repairs progressing. The hole in the front bumper prepared for repair

Nose cone under tray structural repairs being made

Nose cone intake masked off to spray primer paint on under tray to check the quality of the repair

My eldest son, Gregory in body repair mode

My Sprint in the garage nearing completion

Radiator grill and registration numbers yet to be fitted

*My Elan +2 having its coat of many colours
removed back to gel coat*

*The +2 passenger door showing necessary repairs
to the gel coat*

Body paint removed back to gel coat. Front view.

Body paint removed back to gel coat. Rear view

Gel cracks in the front wing identified for subsequent repair

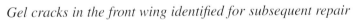

High build and colour primers ready for final rub down

Application of colour final coats

*Take off trailer, pay the bill
(I will do anything except spray paint)*

Custard in the final stages of build

Use of the Professionals

Put body on trailer, take body off trailer. Easy. The hardest part is parting with the cash.

Most people will opt for a professional body shop that has been recommended to them. Ask to see examples of his work, preferably more than two years old, then age defects, if any, will have come to the surface. Restoring and painting GRP bodies is a skill many commercial body shops will not have.

Without making a nuisance of yourself, ask the person responsible for doing your body if you could take photographs for record purposes. He probably will not object as long as you do not interfere with his work. Arrange to take photos at each stage, particularly at the back to glass stage. This proves beyond a shadow of doubt the fact that the preparation was back to glass, the only way.

Storage

If you are not yet ready to position the completed body on the chassis keep it well covered in cotton sheets, free from moisture. It must be able to breath, so do not place polythene sheets directly onto the body. This can cause all sorts of problems with micro blisters and paint discolouration.

Chapter 9

THE ROLLING CHASSIS

Dismantling

The body will be away for some time so take this opportunity to make good use of the space available. This will be the dirtiest part of the whole job, so on with the overalls and get weaving. This is the part of the restoration that can be therapeutic but also exasperating. Parts that have been screwed together for a long time sometimes do not wish to become undone. You have probably come across this already taking the body off. Clean off as much of the accumulated filth as possible. Just an observation, but have you ever stopped to wonder why the maintenance books you have read always show pictures of the strip down of perfectly clean assemblies. Of course they are stage-managed, but in some cases the cars they pull apart are fairly new anyway. You do not have this luxury.

Plusgas penetrating fluid is as good as anything. Liberally soak every nut and bolt with it and leave for at least 24 hours. Now find something else to do.

Engine, Gearbox Removal

While the penetrating fluid is doing its stuff on the rusty bits, turn your attention to the oily bits nestling in the chassis. Remove the exhaust manifold, firstly removing the manifold studs with two $^1/4$ in UNF nuts locked together. The exhaust manifolds can be difficult to remove, particularly with the cylinder head in place and will necessitate the removal of the exhaust side engine mount. With a bit of manoeuvring and patience, they will come out eventually.

Disconnect the clutch hydraulic pipe at the slave

My Elan +2's early rolling chassis. This is an early Lotus replacement ungalvanised example

The same +2 rolling chassis. Fully renovated by myself, adorned by my wife Johanna

My Elan +2. The rolling chassis. The third chassis for this car. A galvanised Lotus replacement with army of body lifters at the ready

The Sprint body removal crew

cylinder. Drain the oil from both the engine and gearbox. Then with suitable lifting gear, and a good length of stout rope wrapped and tied round the engine to enable the hook to be attached in line with the centre of gravity of both engine and box, take the weight of the assembly and remove engine and gearbox mounts. You will appreciate now why the engine and box were left in. Things are much easier to work on as access is now unlimited.

With everything undone lift the assembly, preferably with an assistant to lend a hand. When the sump has cleared the front of the chassis, tilt the engine nose upwards and pull it forward. At this time, ask your assistant to poke his hand through the hole in the side of the chassis and take the weight of the propshaft as it emerges from the back of the gearbox. If you have not drained the gearbox oil this is when

your assistant will cast aspersions as to your lineage. Mop up the oil and continue. A good collection of old rags and a suitable drip tray will not go amiss at this stage. An oil stained garage floor is not good for the finished product.

Wrap a rag around the gearbox end of the drive shaft and tie up in a polythene bag in order to protect the oil seal face. Any damage to the fine-machined surface on this shaft could lead to premature oil seal failure and subsequent oil leak. This is not only unsightly on your new chassis but will make a mess of your drive and will annoy you forever more.

Place the engine and box in a convenient position, cover all holes with tape and plastic bags, and brush the assembly with an oil and grease remover such as Gunk. If the exterior is well laden with sludge,

The early +2 chassis having layers of grime removed

The Sprint rolling chassis strip down was done in two days

scrape off the worst with an old knife or paint scraper first, covering the floor area with newspaper, which should confine most of the debris to the bin. Do not tread it everywhere. Your wife's patience will be well put to the test if you spread this on the best room carpet. When the Gunk has had time to work, hose down and dry off. You will find it much more pleasant working on a clean engine, which in turn will keep your tools, and you, relatively clean.

Engine Strip and rebuild

I do not intend to go into finite detail on engine rebuilds, it is all in the workshop manual, follow it to the letter. Cleanliness and order is the key. Do not rush but think ahead all the time. On rebuild, double-check everything you do. Do not make similar mistakes to the one I made on a rebuild of the +2 engine. With it upturned on the bench, I was just finishing off replacing the sump having torqued up the many little screws. I thought I had done a good job of fitting the sump gaskets, which can be awkward. I stood back reflecting on a job well done when, out of the corner of my eye, perched forlornly at the back of the bench

A Twin Cam engine mounted on an engine stand

was the oil strainer. "Oh my gosh" I said politely. If you believe that you will believe anything!

The engine rebuild will most likely be done simultaneously with all the other work. Just remember to keep dirty work well away from your engine. A true story springs to mind with much relevance. When I used to work for a famous engine manufacturer in East Anglia we were undertaking a comprehensive development programme of a new range of engines. The programme took a set back when a couple of engines went into self-destruct mode on the test bed, which baffled the experts on first strip down inspection.

Finally the engine oil was sent away for analysis. A non-standard constituent was found to be brick dust. On investigation, we found that the builders had been in over the weekend and knocked a hole in the wall. All engines were covered with big plastic sheets and taped up when not being worked on from then on.

Use of an engine stand is ideal and can be used to support the engine by the mounting bosses on the cylinder block. If you have not got an engine stand, position it on a clean board on the garage floor. Chock the sump with suitable blocks of timber to prevent the engine from tipping over and possible damage to the sump, raising the flywheel off the ground.

A work surface with labelled boxes and plastic bags is good practice strategy in order that loose items, nuts, bolts and washers, can be stored ready for cleaning and inspection. Working in such an orderly fashion makes for a well-organised job with less chance of mixing up or just loosing bits.

Starting from the top, remove the eight nuts and washers from the cam cover studs. With a broad blade screwdriver, drive a wedge effect into the four corners of the cam cover gasket. This will destroy the gasket, not that anyone would think of reusing one. Gently twist the screwdriver blade so as not to damage the head and cam cover sealing faces. The cam cover will eventually move and can be pulled clear of the cylinder head. Remove all traces of gasket and remove the rubber 'D' plugs from the camshaft line bores at each end of the cylinder head. Place a ring spanner on the crankshaft pulley bolt head and turn the crankshaft in order that number 1 piston is at top dead centre (TDC) on the compression stroke. Note the timing marks on the camshaft sprockets. With pistons 1 and 4 at TDC, the marks on the two sprockets should be facing each other, level with the top of the cylinder head. With a socket spanner, undo the bolts holding the camshaft sprocket. Unscrew the timing chain tensioner screw by releasing the lock nut and turning the screw anti-clockwise to slacken the chain. Carefully remove the camshaft sprocket bolts complete with lock washers and the large diameter washers. The exhaust sprocket should be marked with the letter X. Pull each sprocket off in turn but be careful that the location dowels at the end of the camshafts do not accidentally drop out and fall into the sump. Allow the timing chain to fall into the head cavity where it will come to rest on the internal water pump cavity housing.

In order to remove the cylinder head; first of all start at the front of the engine at the cylinder head to timing case joint. Slacken off the bolts either side of the timing chest, one from above, the other from below, and slacken off the long bolt at the front of the cylinder head. Remove these bolts and put in a safe place. Remove the camshaft bearing caps from the rear of the inlet camshaft and the front of the exhaust camshaft to give full socket access to the adjacent head bolts. Starting from the outer bolts, the reverse of the head tightening sequence, gradually untighten the cylinder head bolts. Either by using an old head gasket or a cardboard template with holes for accepting the head bolts suitably marked, place each bolt in turn so that it can eventually be returned to the tapped hole it was removed from.

Tap the cylinder head gently under the thermostat housing with a nylon-faced mallet, which should break the head gasket joint. DO NOT TURN the engine in an attempt to break the head gasket joint as a piston may hit valves with dire consequences. Lift the cylinder head off the cylinder block and lay on the bench with a block of wood at each end in order to keep open valves clear of the bench. Cover the cylinder block with cloths and polythene sheets until you are ready to work on it.

Cylinder Head
Measure and record all valve clearances with feeler gauges under the heel of each cam in turn by rotating

the cams to each position. This will necessitate replacing the cam sprockets, washers and bolts in order to do this.

All camshaft bearing caps should be numbered at the factory with corresponding numbers stamped on the head. If not, number every cap and its adjacent posi-

The +2 cylinder head ready for cleanup

tion on the cylinder head. Undo and remove all of these bearing cap nuts and washers and remove the caps with bearings. Remove the camshafts after making sure you have marked one inlet, IN and the exhaust, EX. Remove the camshaft lower bearings and suitably number to ensure they are returned to their original positions if re-used. Remove the cam followers with a suction cup, keeping the associated shims with them. Mark the cam followers with an indelible marker pen 1 – 8 and place in a tin lid.

Turn the head over where you should be able to detect any badly burnt valves, particularly exhaust

The +2 cylinder head ready to go to the machine shop for new valve seat inserts, valve guides and the head face machined flat

The +2 cylinder head from a different angle

valves. Water cooling around the exhaust valve seats is marginal in some areas and often leads to premature exhaust valve burning if the mixture is too lean, and the engine has been worked hard. With a blunt, curved implement, carefully remove excess carbon deposits off the valves and the hemispherical combustion chambers. Be careful not to scrape any aluminium off the head.

Remove all the valves, springs and cotters with a valve spring compressor that has the reach and attachments to access the recessed valve springs

The Sprint cylinder head converted to unleaded petrol

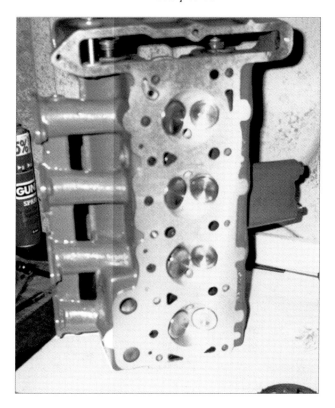

down the cam follower bores in the cylinder head. Sykes Pickervant make a good range of valve spring compressors; these and other suitable tools can be bought from most good motor factors at quite reasonable prices. Do not skimp on this type of tooling as the job is made much easier with the correct tools. Remove all remaining traces of carbon from the inlet and exhaust ports and combustion chambers. Mark the head of each valve with the numbers 1 – 4, "in." or "ex." from the engine front. Keep the spring retainers and cotters with their respective valves.

The +2 head during re-assembly

Inspect the valves for burning and cracking on the seating face, and its relating seat in the cylinder head for undue recession. If any of the valves give cause for concern, discard and replace with new ones. Slight pitting can be removed by lapping in the cylinder head but this should be kept to a minimum to reduce valve seat recession.

Inlet valves usually have a longer life than exhaust valves as they run cooler. Some engine builders will discard exhaust valves as a matter of course as they will not know how long the valves have been in service. They have a reputation to protect and it reduces the risk of warranty claims. Also it means that you do not need to clean up the exhaust valves, a dirty job at the best of times.

If your engine has not been converted to run on lead

free petrol, now may be the time. Take the stripped, bare head to a reputable engine machine shop and get them to replace the valve seats inserts with hardened ones and the cast iron valve guides with phosphor bronze ones. Replace the exhaust valves with the special valves for this service. Your Lotus specialist will be able to advise on the best components for your intended end use, whether it be standard or high performance. Lap in all the valve seats with fine lapping paste until a matt uniform annular ring is observed all round. Clean up everything in petrol and wipe dry. As a final check, engineers blue (a marking paste) can be used to ensure valve seat concentricity.

Assemble the valves and springs back into the cylinder head, coating the valve stems with clean engine oil. Inspect the cam followers for undue wear, particularly the outside diameters for barrelling and excessive rubbing wear pattern of the camshaft contact area. Camshaft followers should rotate by procession as the cam lobe centre is slightly off centre to the cam follower centre. This spreads the wear around the whole top face of the cam follower in contact with the cam lobe. If wear is evidently excessive in the followers and the corresponding sleeves in the cylinder head, then they should all be replaced with new. Again, the services of your engine machine shop will be required to replace the cam follower sleeves.

Inspect each of the tappet shims for excessive indentation and cracking. Measure each one in turn with a micrometer, which should coincide with the factory marking on each shim. Make a note of each shim thickness in the form of a table as shown. Assemble the shims to each of their respective valves followed by the cam followers, all coated in clean engine oil.

Inspect the camshafts and associated bearings for excessive wear and replace as required. If serviceable use the existing camshafts but use new bearings, they are not expensive. Clean everything in petrol and wipe dry, coat with clean engine oil keeping everything spotlessly clean as you proceed. Ensure the camshaft bearing tongues locate in their associated slots in the cylinder head. Coat the camshaft lobes and bearing surfaces with clean engine oil and place into the bearings. Offer up the camshaft sprockets to ensure that the camshafts are in their timing position.

Replace the bearing caps complete with bearings ensuring that the number marked on each cap corresponds with the number marked on the cylinder head. Replace the nyloc nuts with new ones, and with washers underneath tighten down progressively to prevent excessive bending stresses occurring in the camshafts. Camshafts have been known to break if not assembled correctly. Torque the nuts down to the figure quoted in the Service Data.

With each camshaft assembled separately, in order to prevent valve heads from clashing, measure the valve clearances as before. Put these values into the table you made before. If no clearance exists at all due to valve seat recession, fit thinner shims and start again. Shims less than 0.080in are not recommended as they can crack. If the valve clearance is less than the ser-

Valve No	1 IN	1 EX	2 IN	2EX	3 IN	3 EX	4 IN	4 EX
Design Cam Clearance	0.007" 0.005"	0.011" 0.009"	0.007" 0.005"	0.011" 0.009"	0.007" 0.005"	0.011" 0.009"	0.007" 0.005"	0.011" 0.009"
Old Cam Clearance								
Old Shim Thickness								
Difference								
New Shim Thickness								
New Cam Clearance								

N.B. Exhaust cam clearance prior to engine number 9952 was 0.008in/0.006in

vice value, take the difference of the two away from the old shim thickness and obtain a new shim of this thickness. If the valve clearance is more than service clearance, add the difference of the two to the old shim thickness. Reassemble the camshafts as before and check the valve clearances. If all your measurements and calculations are correct, the valve clearances should be right. Loosely fit the camcover to keep out debris. Cover the fully assembled cylinder head in clean rags and put in a safe place until required. Place the head down on two blocks of wood as before to prevent the valves from hitting the bench.

Cylinder Block

Turning your attention to the rest of the engine, remove the distributor, petrol pump, oil pump and the rubber engine breather. Mark the position of the clutch pressure plate with respect to the flywheel with a centre pop and remove by loosening the six retaining screws equally. Make sure that the location dowels in the flywheel do not come loose and fall out. The clutch friction plate will fall out when you remove the pressure plate. Asbestos dust will be present so do not blow the dust away with the risk of inhaling this potentially dangerous substance. Brush gently onto a shovel and throw away. If the clutch has done a high mileage since it was last replaced the

friction face will be very close to the rivets. In any case, do not skimp at this stage of the proceedings as to remove the engine and gearbox soon after you have finished the rebuild just to change a clutch is irritating to say the least. This goes for the clutch pressure plate and spigot bearing as well.

With the clutch dismantled, inspect the flywheel clutch friction face. If it does not show evidence of clutch rivet wear in the form of a large groove or excessive burnishing and cracking of the face then all should be well. If not it may be prudent to have it refaced on a lathe at the engine machine shop. Inspect the starter motor ring gear for burred, worn or broken teeth. If there is any doubt at all have a new one fitted at the engine machine shop. Make sure that the replacement has the same number of teeth as the original or the starter motor will have trouble engaging. Mark the flywheel and crankshaft with a paint mark to ensure that they are re-assembled in their previous position. Remove the six bolts holding the flywheel to the crankshaft. (Four on early Elan engines) These bolts are torqued to very high values and you will need a very good socket of the correct size and probably an extension tube to fit over the socket wench handle. Replace two of the clutch plate retaining screws and with a piece of suitable timber

My Elan +2 cylinder block all cleaned up ready for the machine shop

or a crow bar, provide a torque reaction on the flywheel. With the flywheel removed, two fit people can lift the remaining short engine easily onto the workbench.

If you are not using an engine stand, turn the engine upside down onto its head face with the timing chain rubbing strip hanging over the edge of the bench and proceed to remove the sump. Place all the screws and washers into a tin so that none are lost. Tap the side of the sump flange with a nylon faced mallet that should loosen it. If you have to use wedges, be careful not to distort or damage the sealing faces. Remove the sump with all traces of gasket material and jointing compound.

The sludge at the base of the sump will indicate what sort of life the engine has been subjected to. Lots of metallic swarf-like material will mean heavy piston and bearing wear. Remnants of timing chain rollers and the odd gear tooth and washer or two will mean that the car has been handled by unsympathetic people. Consistent black oil with no gritty bits felt between thumb and forefinger means that the engine has had a good life.

Next remove the front timing cover noting where all the different lengths of bolts fit. Pull off the front cover, noting the water pump impeller and insert. No matter what condition the water pump is in, replace the internals at every occasion the head and sump are removed. They are cheap Ford bits but only have a limited life in the Lotus front cover. Follow the instructions in the workshop manual to the letter but note that modern kits do not have a flinger, which can be ignored. At the same time, replace the timing chain rubbing strip if deeply grooved. Remove the jackshaft dummy camshaft by first lifting the locking washer tabs. Undo the single screw holding the timing cover back plate to the cylinder block, remove and clean off all traces of gasket and sealant. Undo the jackshaft retaining fork bolts and remove fork and jackshaft.

Remove the rear crankshaft oil seal housing and take out the old oil seal, cleaning off all traces of gasket and sealant. Replace the oil seal with a new one, ensuring it is pushed into its correct axial position. This will put the seal lip in the original position on the crankshaft ensuring oil tightness. Do the same with the oil seal in the front cover.

The cylinder block is now down to its very basics and in order to strip down further, remove the oil pick up

The +2 crank, rods and pistons ready for cleanup and inspection

pipe complete with strainer and the oil return pipe. Turn the cylinder block the right way up, positioned on blocks of wood to keep the crankshaft clear of the bench if not using an engine stand. Mark each piston top with its cylinder number and an arrow marked front. This will probably already be stamped on the piston crowns by the manufactures. Invert the cylinder block and mark each big end and main bearing cap with centre pop dots if not already done so, to ensure that they are returned to their original position. Undo each of the big end bolts and remove each big end cap with bearing in turn. Turn the block on its end using blocks of wood if done on the bench to clear the crankshaft. Push each piston and con rod assembly through the top of the cylinder block.

Keep each piston, rod and bearing assembly together on the bench so as to clearly identify the one that relates to each cylinder. Remove the pistons from their respective con rods by removing the circlip from one side of the gudgeon pin with a good set of circlip pliers. The gudgeon pin should be a hand push fit into the piston. If it proves a little tight put them in the oven at 50°C. Protecting your hands with a rag, the gudgeon pin should push out easily. Clean the carbon off the top of the piston but do not remove all the carbon from above the top ring. If the piston is to be re-used, this carbon ring provides an elementary oil seal.

Give the pistons an initial inspection for obvious defects, which would make further cleaning a waste of time. Any scuffing on the sides of the pistons would render them unserviceable. Inspect the cylinder bores for tram-lining and excessive lip at the point where the top ring reaches its upper limit. If you have access to internal micrometers then check the cylinder bores to gauge whether or not they are within service tolerances. If they are not, then a re-bore and new pistons are in order.

Lotus recommended that a re-bore of 0.015in was the maximum but pistons up to 0.040in oversize can now be obtained. When going out to this size, I would recommend that the bores are checked for porosity as blowholes in the cylinder walls due to casting imperfections can cause water leakage from the water jacket into the cylinder. If this does occur then the cylinder block can be re-sleeved. My +2 engine was re-sleeved after burning a piston top when it was already

on the maximum oversize of +0.040in. It is now back to standard bore of 3.250in giving the original engine capacity of 1,558cc. That was the price paid for giving a 3-litre Injection Capri a good run for his money around the M25 at 3am one Sunday morning on returning from a trip to France. One lives and learns.

If the pistons look in good condition with visible machining marks all round, and the cylinder bores are all within tolerance, then this is evidence of an exceptionally low-mileage, well-looked after engine. It could be that it had just been rebuilt prior to being laid up. Either way, you are lucky and money is saved. If in any doubt though, replace with new parts and, in any case, renew the piston rings as a matter of course.

Lastly, undo the main bearing cap retaining bolts and then remove each cap in turn complete with bearings, including the thrust bearings at the centre web position. Before removing the thrust bearing, check for end float with a dial test indicator at the end of the crankshaft. If the end float is outside of service tolerances, then the thrust washers must be replaced.

Lift out the crankshaft and clean thoroughly in petrol ensuring that all oil ways are clean and blown out with compressed air. Inspect the plain bearing journals of both big ends and mains. Any signs of scuffing, pick-up, or general signs of wear render them useless. For the price of these plain bearings I would recommend that they be replaced anyway. "Don't spoil the ship for ha'path of tar".

Visually inspect the crankshaft journals for obvious signs of wear. Blueing, scuffing, spalling, pick-up and tram-lining are all defects that can be recognised with the naked eye. If the crankshaft looks fine, measure each journal with a micrometer to assess its serviceability. If you have not got the instruments or the knowledge to do this for yourself, take the crank to your engine machine shop and ask them to do it for you. If the crankshaft is in need of a regrind, ensure that the machine shop is clued up on all things Lotus and is knowledgeable of the radius runouts as shown in the diagram of the crankshaft.

Clean all engine components spotless and lay out on the bench on clean paper towelling. Replace the main bearings into the cylinder block ensuring that both sides of the bearings are smeared in clean engine oil. This precaution prevents corrosion and galling of the steel bearing backing. Make sure that the oil holes in the bearings are in line with the oil holes in the cylinder block and that the tongues in the bearings sit in the slots machined for them in the cylinder block. Smear plenty of clean engine oil on the crankshaft journals and position the crank in the cylinder block. Place in position the thrust bearings at the centre bearing position and then replace the main bearing caps complete with plain bearings.

A timely check is to ensure that the bearings you are about to fit on the crankshaft are of the correct size. Mistakes have been known to be made with bearings being supplied of the wrong size. This can either cause the crank to be dead tight, which is obvious from the outset, or worse still the bearings being too large a diameter which could go unnoticed until you come to start the engine, when a horrible knocking sound which is unmistakable emanates from the sump.

Make sure that all the main bearing caps are replaced in their correct positions, the right way round. This is normally marked on the caps by cast embossed arrows pointing to the front of the engine. If the engine is to be used for any competition or performance work, use new main bearing and big end bolts. For normal use the bolts can be re-used but check them carefully for any signs of stretching, thread deformation or cracking under the bolt head.

Lubricate the threads of all main bearing and big end bolts. Tighten the big end bolts, one cap at a time and check at each one that the crankshaft is still free to rotate. Torque up to the service torque figure with a good fitting socket and a torque wrench. If the crankshaft is difficult to rotate, check the bearings are of the right size, no high spots exist, or any dirt has got in between bearings, shells or caps. Cleanliness is essential to avoid this sort of problem that can be exasperating and if goes unnoticed will result in shortened engine life.

Assemble the pistons back to their respective conrods ensuring that the pistons are the right way round. Position the piston ring gaps 120° apart and assemble a piston ring compressor around the piston to close up the rings to enable the pistons to be pushed back into their bores. Smear clean engine oil in the bores, the pistons and small end bushes. Push the pistons back into the cylinder block, compressing the piston rings with the compressor sufficient to just allow the piston to move within it. A knock with a wooden hammer shaft may be needed to encourage the piston to finally enter its bore. Do not apply too great a force or you may crack a piston ring with disastrous results.

Carefully locate each conrod in turn onto its respective crank journal with big end shell in position. Rotate the crankshaft to access the big end cap replacement and bolt up each cap in turn with bearing shells well lubricated and positioned correctly. Torque up with the torque wrench to the service torque figure. Turn the crankshaft by hand to ensure that all is well and that each piston goes up and down without any problems. The rotating/reciprocating assembly may appear a little stiff if new bearings and pistons have been fitted. This is quite normal until everything has had a chance to bed in. As long as you can turn the crankshaft by the balancing webs, all should be well. If it is dead tight, investigate. Caps in the wrong position, undersized bearings, rods and pistons mixed up, any one of these mistakes and more can cause untold problems. Patience, cleanliness, being methodical and sure of what you are doing are all essential factors of a good engine rebuild. Unless you get all these factors right at this stage of the process, you are wasting your time and money.

Inspect the jackshaft bearings in the cylinder block for undue wear. They do not do much in the way they were originally designed for, i.e. camshaft operation via push rod, as in Ford Kent guise so they generally wear quite well. Replace the jackshaft from the front of the engine and bolt up the thrust washer fork. Replace the rear crankshaft oil seal and bolt up, torque the bolts up to the service torque.

Replace the front cover back plate after first smearing the joint faces with a thin smear of silicon sealant. Use of this material will give some reassurance of oil tightness but must be used sparingly. Any excess oozing inside the engine can cause havoc with oil strainers, bearings, oil pump, etc.

Bolt this back cover to the cylinder block with the single bolt, making sure that the sump joint faces are level. The top face will be slightly below the level of the top face of the cylinder block. This is to make room for the cork gasket in front of the head gasket. Replace the jackshaft sprocket, not forgetting to replace the locking tab washer with a new one. Replace the oil suction pipe, strainer and oil return pipe.

Assemble a new endless timing chain over the crankshaft sprocket and fit the oil slinger over the end of the crankshaft nose. Smear a thin film of silicon sealant on to the gasket faces and also in the recess for the water pump adapter. Offer up the front timing cover with new water pump internals and feed the timing chain inside the flange faces. Insert all the bolts, nuts, and screws into their original locations and tighten up to their recommended torque figures ensuring that the sump flange faces are in line.

Position the sump gaskets on to the sump face of the cylinder block with a thin smear of silicon sealant. Locate the cork or sometimes rubber strips in the slots at the front and rear oil seal bosses and cut to length as recommended in the workshop manual to ensure compression against the sump gasket. Again, a thin smear of silicon sealant will ensure oil tightness.

Offer the sump onto the gasket and push down carefully and evenly so as not to disturb the gaskets. Insert a number of screws to engage with the holes in the gaskets and eventually into the tapped holes in the cylinder block, front and rear covers. Pull down gently and insert all of the remaining screws. Screw down all screws evenly and finally torque down to the service torque.

Assembling Cylinder Head to Cylinder Block
It is essential to use two long studs to locate the cylinder head as it is placed on top of the cylinder block. These can be made up from two old head bolts by cutting off the heads and saw cutting a screwdriver slot in the top. Place the two studs diametrically opposed to each other. Place the head gasket in position over the studs ensuring that the gasket is the right way up. Position the cork gasket on top of the timing case using a thin film of silicon sealant on both sides of the gasket. Push a new rubber crankcase breather into the cylinder block with again, a thin film of silicon sealant top and bottom.

With the camshafts in their timing position, i.e.

sprocket markings facing each other, and with the crankshaft at TDC position as indicated by the notch in the crankshaft pulley coinciding with the TDC mark on the front of the timing chain cover, lift the cylinder head over the two studs and feed down gently. With both camshaft sprockets removed, ensure that the timing chain tensioner sprocket is free to move and will engage with the timing chain. Make sure as well that the crankcase breather is well seated in the under side of the cylinder head as this is a very common area for aggravated oil leaks which are difficult to fix without removing the cylinder head, so get it right now. Screw the head bolts in to their previous positions, which you should have identified from your early template or disused head gasket. Ensure the bolts are spotlessly clean, free from all carbon, burnt oil, corrosion and defective thread form. Any doubts on the condition of these bolts then replace. Lightly oil the threads and plain diameters before inserting into the head. Take out the two locating studs when the other bolts are firmly in position and replace with the remaining two head bolts. Remove the same camshaft bearing caps as before to gain full access to the head bolt with the socket spanner. Tighten the head bolts gradually in the sequence as shown in the workshop manual. As you are doing this replace the two bolts either side of the timing case and the long bolt at the centre position.

Torque the head bolts up to the service torque in increments. First 20lb.ft., then 40 and finally 60–65lb.ft. Always work in the diagonal sequence starting from the centre as shown in the workshop manual or there is a good risk of the cylinder head becoming distorted with subsequent head gasket failure. Tighten up the front three bolts between the timing case and cylinder head and replace the cam bearing caps. Pull up the timing chain with a bent wire; wire coat hangers are a versatile garage tool. Ensure it is fully engaged with the crankshaft and chain tensioner sprockets by rotating the crank slowly back and forth with a spanner on the crankshaft pulley bolt.

Make sure that the crankshaft is at the TDC position and then position the timing chain over the camshaft sprocket location diameters. With a sprocket in each hand, feed the chain onto the sprocket teeth, keeping the timing marks facing each other, locating the sprockets onto their location diameters and timing pegs. This can be perfected with practice but is not easy. Do not expect to get it right first time. Note the position of the timing marks on the sprockets. No matter what the workshop manual says, you will never get them perfectly in line. By trial and error you will get them as near as you can. It will come to you eventually. Bolt up the sprockets and torque up to the service torque aided with a spanner on the crankshaft pulley bolt. To get the marks to locate perfectly, some after market manufacturers sell vernier adjustable sprockets but unless you are looking for that last bit of extra horsepower, do not bother. Tension the chain to give 0.5in total up and down movement on the top run by turning the tensioner screw clockwise. Turn the engine over a couple of turns by hand ensuring all is well then recheck the timing chain adjustment. When satisfied, nip up the locknut on the tensioner screw.

Liberally oil all the cams and bearings keeping oil off the cam cover sealing faces. Put in place the rubber 'D' seals at the camshaft line bores at the ends of the cylinder head, making sure that the pips sit in the holes at the base of the half moons. Apply a thin film of silicon sealant under these 'D' seals, the cam cover face on the head and on the cam cover itself. Carefully put in place the cam cover gasket on the head face and offer up the cam cover and press down gently. Make sure that the gasket is flush with the outer face all round and has not been pushed in. Lotus used copper washers in an attempt to seal the cam cover studs but these days you can get hold of rubber coated washers that are far superior. They can only be used once though. Use new nyloc nuts and tighten them all in sequence progressively to ensure that the cover sits down parallel. Tighten the nuts eventually to the service torque figure. Do not be tempted to tighten them any further. A distorted cam cover will result in possible extrusion of the gasket and inevitable oil leaks. An oil tight twin cam engine is not impossible but takes care and patience. Some engine builders will prefer the use of other proprietary sealants but the correct use of whichever system you choose is imperative in order to achieve the desired results.

Reassemble the flywheel back on the crankshaft in the same position it was removed, and tighten the bolts up to the service torque. Build up the clutch, preferably with the use of a clutch centralising tool. This makes it much easier to align the splines properly with the centre of the flywheel thus making the mating up to the gearbox much easier.

With the crankshaft undisturbed in the timing position, now is the time to fit the distributor. Turn the crankshaft pulley back to the static ignition timing position. The ignition leads from the distributor cap should be pointing to the rear of the engine and the rotor arm in the distributor alongside the electrode for number one cylinder. Turn the distributor shaft clockwise 45° to compensate for the movement of the helical gear on the jackshaft. Using a multi-meter or a battery and 12-volt bulb, time the ignition by turning the distributor so the bulb light is extinguished or the circuit broken. My experience with static timing in this manner has had quite good results.

If the engine has done a high mileage, then a new oil pump and petrol pump should be fitted. Re-using old indeterminate ancillaries is false economy and will eventually lead to frustrating breakdowns.

Drive Train Removal
Again, this is quite straightforward if you follow the workshop manual. When the manual states that the differential only comes out one side, believe it. Mark the mating flanges at the differential and propshaft with a centre pop to ensure they go back in the same way. This eliminates a possible source of vibration.

Removal of old drive shaft Metalastik doughnut couplings can be a nightmare if they have been in-situ for ages. Again, patience will prevail. Attach large jubilee clips to each coupling in turn and compress the coupling in order to take the load off the fixing bolts. If the bolts have seized in the bosses of the couplings, soak in penetrating fluid and leave for 24 hours. If the couplings have seen a lot of service they will be badly split and could break up in attempting to undo the bolts. If that is the case, separate them with a sharp knife, uncoupling the shafts and dismantle on the bench in a more comfortable position.

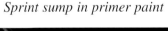

Sprint sump in primer paint

Completed Sprint engine

Drive Train Strip and rebuild

Follow the cleaning procedure as for the engine and box. Remove the inboard drive shafts with a slide hammer, having first removed the circlips retaining the bearings. Have you drained the oil first? Gear oil is smelly stuff. These bearings will probably be well embedded in the casing. Do not abuse the shafts, or the casing, they are expensive to replace. A little bit of heat and/or Plus Gas usually does the trick.

Remove the differential from the casing and inspect for backlash and wear. Inspect the casing for cracks at the mounting bosses. A hint here, very few people have the where-with-all to rebuild and set up a differential properly. I have done it once and was lucky that the input bearings did not need replacing. A special jig is required in order to set up the gears correctly. A transmission specialist is far better equipped and trained to do this work, which will not break the bank.

A noisy differential is to be avoided at all costs if you do not want a constant headache when driving. It is also difficult to remove with the body in-situ. The output shaft bearings require a press to remove and replace without risk of damage to the shafts. A specialist will do this for you at very little cost, as long as you buy the bearings from him in the first place.

The same goes for the gearbox. A four-speed unit can be completely over-hauled by a specialist at quite modest costs and it will be right. Five-speed units I would not like to comment on, not ever having had one.

The drive shaft universal joints should be replaced as a matter of course. They are very cheap, but again, not a job you want to do lightly once the body is back on. Have the shaft balanced as well, which will increase your confidence in a smooth ride.

Rear Suspension Removal

The Chapman struts at the rear of the car are quite straightforward and necessitate nothing more than a good set of coil spring compressors. With the chassis off the ground, chocked up on axle stands and timber, unless you have any more off cuts of railway sleepers, remove the rear wheels. Undo the centre nuts on the outboard drive shafts and remove the hubs. Easy isn't it. No it is not, for a hub that has been coupled to a drive shaft on a slow taper for eons does not want to come apart. Do not attempt to extract the hub with massive legged hydraulic pullers, you will bend the hub flange.

Take a trip to your now friendly Lotus specialist and ask for a rear hub puller. It is a very simple bit of kit, not expensive and every Elan owner should have one. Now is the time.

All this can be done on the bench if you have a big enough vice, once you have separated the damper and rear wishbones from the chassis.

Rear Suspension Strip and rebuild

You will now have realised the importance of soaking all the old nuts and bolts with penetrating fluid. If the car has been sadly neglected for a long period, the bolts holding the A frames to the uprights will be seized in due to dissimilar metal corrosion. Do not use large amounts of force to remove, as you will probably crack the upright bosses. Use copious amounts of penetrating fluid and leave for a further 24 hours, dry off then apply judicious heat from a gas torch. If the bolt heads are of the thin, cut-down variety in order to clear the wheel rims, be extra careful, as they will not accept large amounts of torque without taking the flats off. If you are lucky, the bolts should now turn in the housing and can be worked loose to remove. A last resort is the hacksaw.

As you can probably appreciate from the last paragraph, patience pays off in the end, and no more so than working on an old Lotus. Do not attempt to rush this kind of job but think it through. It will pay dividends in the end. The job will not be bodged, nothing will get broken and you will stand less chance of having bruised or bleeding knuckles.

Front Suspension, Steering Removal
The same remarks as for the rear suspension apply just as well. Follow the workshop manual to the letter and use lots of patience.

Front Suspension, Steering Strip and rebuild
The front suspension is remarkably similar to a Triumph Herald. In fact, most of it is derived from the Herald/Vitesse family of saloons. The main differences are the suspension arms, springs and dampers. The arms are lightweight pressings, which will not take much mal-treatment. The lower damper mounting bolt could be loose and subsequently elongated the holes in the arms, causing stress cracks along the way. If the arms are badly corroded, disfigured, bent, have elongated holes and cracks, discard. Lotus replacement arms are now reinforced in these areas

The +2 front suspension prior to the first restoration

Goosed chassis was cut up ready for the skip. Body is on off cuts of railway sleepers

as this was considered to be a common fault. These suspension arm fixings should be torqued up to the recommended settings and rechecked at frequent intervals to prevent this from happening. Never place a jack under these front suspension arms.

Steering components are commonplace and should be replaced if found to be suspect, as they probably will be. The steering rack is not a straightforward Triumph item. It is specifically modified by Lotus to include lock limiter spacers that are essential for the operation and safety of the Elan.

Chassis – Refurbish or Replace

Should the chassis be the original or a non-galvanised early replacement, discard it. It will be highly unlikely that an original chassis will have lasted the rigours of time, even if it looks serviceable.

New Lotus galvanised chassis ready for rebuild. My youngest son, Matthew looks on attentively

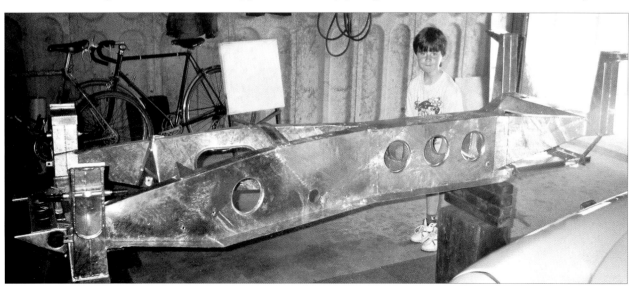

The Sprints rolling chassis

Front and rear turrets are prone to corrosion from the inside, leading to considerable weakening of these vital areas. Also stress cracking can occur at the rear suspension mounting points whereby the A frames can become detached from the chassis. Rear wheel steering on the throttle is sound evidence that all is not well at the rear end. This happened to me in my +2 before I changed the chassis for the last time and believe me, it is a most unnerving experience.

If it is a genuine Lotus galvanised unit, look for erosion and possible corrosion of the underside. If it appears to be accident free and not twisted in any way, have it checked out by a specialist. Remember, you bought this car as a rebuild project, unless you are extremely lucky and some one has recently fitted a new chassis using all the old un-restored running gear, then the chassis is probably well passed its best. The original makers can repair a Spyder chassis with front-end damage but you have to ask yourself if this is what you want.

Chapter 10

PREPARATION FOR THE REBUILD

Make a List

By this time you will have a good idea of what parts you wish to replace with new, and the parts that are worth renovating. Make a list and shop around to ensure that the parts are available, at what cost and whether they are on back order at the factory. Some parts may be discontinued and you may be left with making the best out of what you have got, or search the small ads in Lotus club magazines. Some parts can be obtained at autojumbles, especially at Lotus events around the country. A word of warning, there is a lot of rubbish about so be selective. Know exactly what you want and how much you are prepared to pay. Some parts though will command a high price if rare and in good condition.

Reverse all Strip Down Instruction – The Great Manual Get Out Clause

All workshop manuals seem to rely on this method of rebuild instruction. It saves on print and paper, but is no help to you when no way will an assembly go back together the way it came apart. In some cases things have a habit of falling apart when you least expect it and the manual description is meaningless. Remember the photographs you took a while back? Dig them out and see if any you took have some bearing on the problem in hand. If you took adequate notes and made sketches at the time these might be of some help. This is the time when you wish you had made sketches, took more photographs, but hindsight is a great leveller. When you do start to strip anything, think. Will you be able to rebuild it in two years time when you have forgotten every thing you did at the time?

Cleanliness is the Key

Back to the rebuild, everything now is ready for the big re-assembly. This is what you have been aiming for over the last few months or even longer. Look around you. Is the garage clean and tidy? Can you eat your dinner off the floor? If not, you need to embark on a more rigorous cleaning regime. All right, perhaps I am being a little fussy, but I cannot over emphasise the advantages of having a clean and tidy environment in which to work in. If nothing else it will reflect in the finished product, your car.

You have your new shiny galvanised chassis, do you paint it or just rust protect it. This is entirely up to you. If you want to retain originality, a liberal coating of corrosion protection wax all over is recommended. If you intend to use the car all year round in salt, slush and anything else that the British weather can throw at it, then consult a paint specialist. Some marine paint systems have been used in the past but remember that before painting galvanised steel, a special acid etch process has to be applied first.

A stove enamelled finish over a fully prepared galvanised chassis is a good option and is used extensively by professional restorers. Spyder prefer to rely on stove enamelling as it is much easier to repair a non-galvanised section by welding.

Chapter 11

THE ROLLING CHASSIS REBUILD

Start Up-Side Down
The easiest way to start a chassis rebuild is the wrong way up. This enables you to attach brake-pipes in comfort. Raise the chassis on stands, blocks, Work-mates, etc, to a comfortable height. This will take the strain off your back and make things much easier to see. The chassis at this stage only weighs about 75 pounds, light enough for two people to move around with ease.

Corrosion Protection, Do it Now
All of the running gear and suspension arms will require re-bushing. Even if not evidently broken or badly deformed, rubber does age and loses its elastic properties. This will show up in a spongy ride and inferior handling.

After removing all rubber bushes from the suspension arms, remove all old paint, grease, oil and rust. Plenty of elbow grease or the use of a good grit blaster is recommended. Paint all non-mating surfaces with a good paint system of your choice. Some people will recommend two pack paints, others powder coatings. Certain two pack paint systems can be more durable and abrasion resistant but others prefer the impact resistance of the powder coatings. There is not a lot to choose between the two.

Use of copper grease is strongly recommended for all screw, nut and bolt fixings. If at a later date you have to dismantle parts, they will unscrew that much easier.

Work in an Orderly Fashion – Be Prepared
When rebuilding, lay out all the components along the side of the chassis you are working on. Ensure that any handed parts, that is, left or right hand are on the correct side. Only use new nuts, bolts and washers. A tip here, most specialists will offer you a complete set of fixings for the whole car, sourced by them for the job in hand, bagged and labelled for your convenience. Buy them. This will save you a lot of time and frustration in obtaining imperial size fixings, because in case you have not noticed, the rest of the world has gone metric.

Brake Pipes, Hand brake cable and petrol pipe
First thing to fix to the chassis are the hydraulic brake

Suspension arms and driveshaft laid out for inspection. The long lower arms were replaced with new ones

The build starts. The long brake pipe has already been fitted with the chassis upside down.

The rear end takes shape. Note the hand brake "tree" behind the differential

pipes running from front to back. The copper/nickel variety are best as they are more corrosion resistant, harder than pure copper and will sustain a polish finish longer. Never fit steel brake pipes, they will rust through eventually. This is another job you only want to do once. Plastic protection strips can be used here to provide added protection to the chassis and pipes at the brake pipe clamping strips.

While the chassis is free of all obstructions, fit the hand brake cable and the petrol pipe, ensuring that the petrol pipe is clipped to the underside of the chassis top with enough free length either end to cut off later. If you have ever tried to fit these items with the body in place and all running gear fitted you will know why I have made an issue of the point at this stage.

The Hand Brake Tree

The Elan hand brake system is the most misunderstood mechanism in the world. If fitted correctly it works, and not just for MOT time.

Attach the handbrake tree mechanism making sure it is well lubricated with grease. If you are clever here it is possible to use modified spacers, a cap headed screw and washers that will enable you to remove the retaining bolt under the differential if need be in the future. This job can usually only be done with the body off or by cutting a hole in the front of the boot. The secret is to extend the rear spacer till it penetrates the rear A frame lug so that a spanner can be located on the nut fixed onto the cap headed screw. This can be achieved with the body in position and the mechanism dismantled with some dexterity without having to cut holes in the body.

Mounting the Differential

Bolt on to the chassis the differential mountings and the rear suspension uprights rubber mountings.

Then offer up the differential assembly to the chassis. Patience is needed here, as it will only go back the way it came out. Believe me, it will go back, unless

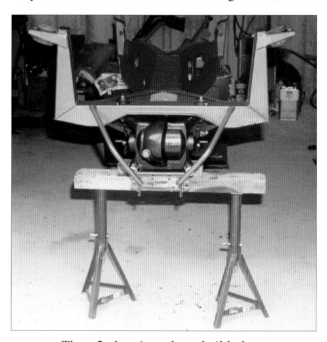

The +2 chassis under rebuild phase

your chassis has been dropped from a great height or run over by a double deck bus without you noticing. Add the differential tie rods with new rubber bushes and fasten their ends to the chassis utilising the special tapered nuts and locknuts for this purpose. Use of any other method of attaching these rods will result in a lot of clanking at the rear end and eventual damage to the chassis. Fill to the bottom of the oil inlet hole with EP 90 gear oil. It will never be any easier to do this than now.

The Rear Suspension

Build the rear suspension as per the workshop manual remembering not to torque up any of the nuts and bolts as this is one of the last things to be done at the

Rear suspension 'A' frames being cleaned up prior to rebushing

end of the rebuild to ensure correct chassis ride height. Liberal coating of copper grease on all nuts and bolts at this point will ensure that you never have the dismantling problems you encountered earlier.

The Drive Train

From the front of the chassis, feed in the newly renovated propshaft and position at the differential drive flange to the marks previously made on strip down. This will ensure that the driveshaft takes up the same orientation on rebuild. Attach with new nuts, bolts and washers and tighten up to the recommended torque. Wrap a rag around the gearbox end of the driveshaft and tie up in a polythene bag in order to protect the oil seal diameter as before until it is time to install the engine and gearbox.

The Front Suspension

Molten zinc will almost certainly have encroached onto the wishbone mounting spindles and even into the screw threads on a galvanised chassis. Clean off any un-wanted zinc with emery paper and run a die

The +2 anti-roll bar bush showing the reason for a lot of clunking

Steering takes shape

down each of the spindles before attempting to attach the wishbones to the chassis. Smother these spindles in copper grease. Attach the lower and upper wishbones to the chassis, followed by the large retention washers and nyloc nuts. Mount the spring/damper units to the front turrets and then attach to the lower wishbones.

Front springs and dampers assembled

The front end is nearly there. Note the large diameter washers on the front suspension arm pivots.
These keep the arms tied to the chassis if the rubber bushes give way

When I stripped the front suspension on the +2 for the first time, I was horrified to find that the rubber bushes in the suspension arms had long since lost their rubber. Being new to the car, I could not explain all the noise at the front end until I removed these nuts and large washers. The washers hid the offending bushes but also prevented the arms from falling off the chassis. New bushes all round cured the noise problem and the handling of the car improved noticeably.

Build the front suspension as per the workshop manual remembering not to torque up any of the nuts and bolts as this is one of the last things to be done at the end of the rebuild to ensure correct chassis ride height.

Mount the lower trunnions to the lower wishbones with the uprights attached, ensuring a good covering of the swivel threads in EP90 gear oil. Do not use any kind of grease in the steering swivels. It will go hard and eventually make the steering stiff. In extreme circumstances, the threads will wear to such an extent that they will pull out of the lower trunnion and you will lose a front wheel. This is most likely to happen on full lock but even so it can do a lot of damage.

Attach the upper ball joints to the steering uprights and bolt up to the upper wishbones.

Steering
The steering rack, as mentioned previously, is a modified Triumph unit with internal spacers added to limit the lock. The height that the rack is mounted on the chassis is critical in order to avoid bump steer. This is achieved at the factory by arriving at shim thickness that are marked on the chassis. It is imperative to position these shims under the rack.

Hubs and Brakes
Rear brake discs are special to Lotus, as are the rear brake calipers. The brake discs out of true run out, as measured with a dial test indicator on the disc face should not exceed 0.004in. The rear brake discs can produce a phenomenon that gives an impression that a fault occurs with the front brakes. This is caused by out of true rear discs wearing in such a way as to produce a wavy washer effect. Actual variation in disc thickness can be measured at various positions around the disc. This induces pressure variations in the hydraulic circuit that is then transferred to the front brake cylinders. I changed the front discs on my +2 before I realised it was the rear discs that were causing the problem.

Rear discs running out of true can be caused by any number of factors, such as drive shaft irregularities, spiders bent out of true due to amateurish wheel bearing replacements, dirt on mating faces or distorted discs. Shimming true brake discs can be done but requires expert technical knowledge and is not recommended to the uninitiated. If you have any suspicions about the serviceability of any of the brake discs, replace with new ones.

Front discs are much more straightforward being of basic Triumph design mounted on a conventional hub. As such they are much cheaper. The brake pads are not of Triumph origin and it is essential to use the recommended pad material for your vehicle, the main difference being hard pads for servo applications and soft pads for non- servo vehicles.

Wheel hubs are the most important items to get handed correctly at the start. One side has left hand threads for the wheel spinners, and the other side right hand. Consult the workshop manual, for which is which. If you get it wrong the wheels fall off. Now go and order that workshop manual.

Engine and Gearbox

Get these in before the body is attached to the chassis for the last time. See fitting the body. As before, do not attach the heater valve to the cylinder head until the body is in place. Sling the engine and box as for removing and offer into position, raised at the front. Feed the gearbox quill shaft extension into the chassis box section. At the same time, ask an assistant to feed the propshaft nose into the gearbox as the engine is being lowered into position. Attach the gearbox mount under the box and the engine mounts to the engine. Lower gently into position. This translates roughly to "If you can get the engine and mounts to pass the chassis engine mounting brackets without a lot of cussing and swearing please let me know". This again is where the Lotus virtue of "patience" comes into its own.

On the baby Elan, the tall engine mount should be on the left, looking from the front, the standard mount on the other side. This is to give the carburettors clearance over the inner body. On the +2 they are both standard as adequate clearance exists. Bolt up the mounts to the engine and chassis and also the

Engine in situ. The unrestored wheels are on early Dunlop SP Sports tyres. Well past their best

The completed front end with engine in place. Note the cut out profile in the chassis to clear the exhaust manifold. Powder coated wheels are now shod with Dunlop SP10's

gearbox mount. Fill both with oil as per the workshop manual. Ensure the drain plugs are fitted first. You would not be the first to put a gallon of engine oil over the garage floor.

Exhaust

At this stage it is prudent to fit the exhaust manifold to the engine as you are fitting the engine mounts. One or both of the manifold downpipes will probably foul with the chassis. Mark the chassis with a felt tip pen to give 5mm clearance round the pipes. Remove the pipes and then file out the profile required and round off all edges and corners. This will enhance manifold removal in service as well as preventing the risk of damaging the pipes and an awful noise generator to boot. Treat the exposed metal surfaces with rust inhibiting wax.

It is virtually impossible to fit an Elan manifold over the exhaust studs, so take the studs out with two $1/4$ in UNF nuts locked together, then re-insert when the manifold and gaskets are in position. If you think this

is difficult, wait for the time when you have to remove the manifolds with the body in position. You will become an expert in Chinese wire puzzles overnight.

Once the manifold is fixed to the head, fit the right hand side engine mount.

Ancillaries

At this stage, fit the starter motor and clutch cylinder while they are easy to get at. Removing and refitting an Elan starter motor on a fully assembled car is an experience that most Elan owners will have to do sooner or later. With a trained eye, practiced dexterity and the educated use of the socket set, it can be done. Practice this now and try to visualise the body, carburettors and other ancillaries in your way. Remember it well, you will thank me for this one.

The Elan starter motor is based on the Mk 1 Cortina engine, as is the cylinder block. The two starter motor fastening fixing bolts had a notorious habit of shaking themselves loose on these engines, my Mk 1

Completed rolling chassis. Note the engine wrapped up to keep out the dirt

Cortina certainly did. In extreme circumstances the motor could fall off or break off the flange lugs of the starter motor. The problem still exists to this day on Elans and is easily overcome by fitting large 3mm thick steel washers with lock washers under each of the bolt heads. Ensure that the Bendix and ring gear have not been damaged first. Any suspect components should be replaced.

Helping to change an Elan starter motor on a travelling companions car in the middle of France in the pouring rain at the side of the road was an experience I would rather forget.

Even Ford can get it wrong as I found out when I changed the Mk 1 for the Mk 2 1600E. The starter motor now had an extra bolt in the flange. As it was, Lotus never did incorporate this later modification.

The +2 rolling chassis

Wheels and Tyres

Steel wheels should be checked for running true, corrosion and splits and replaced or repaired as required. Paint finish choice is yours, but I would recommend powder coating finished off with lacquer. Wheel embellishers are readily available and add that finishing touch. Chromed rim +2 wheels are hard to source but if they are sound wheels, sand blasting and powder coating is recommended. MGB wheel embellishers will fit and look the part if the chrome is in a bad state.

Aluminium wheels of the type fitted to the +2 are available from time to time from specialists. Original aluminium wheels should be inspected for bead face damage, corrosion, cracking and porosity. If

The +2 rolling chassis from another angle

you are to fit aluminium wheels to an Elan, be aware that the spinners are different to the steel wheel type.

Spinners can be re-profiled and re-chromed if not too badly damaged by careless owners, but again, new ones are readily available.

There is a vast selection of tyres to choose from for the Elan and the +2. Original fitments are no longer available from the OEM manufacturers. Dunlop SP Sports with the original tread pattern are available from specialist manufacturers but are not cheap. Never fit a hard, non-compliant tyre to a baby Elan if you intend to be ever caught in the rain. They

The +2 rolling chassis – gearbox in place

will cover a decent mileage on a +2 but be careful in the wet. All other manufacturers will market something that will fit but personal preference will play a large part in your choice. If you want maximum grip under all conditions then choose a soft rubber compound tyre, but do not expect a high mileage from them. I have fitted modern Dunlop SP 10s to my Sprint, which cover my needs. I know a few other people who have fitted them to Elans without complaint.

Wheels should be accurately balanced and rechecked at frequent intervals in order to avoid accelerated wear to steering and suspension components. Out of balance wheels can affect the whole nature of the car and make it unpleasant to drive.

I needed to buy a couple of replacement wheels for the +2 a number of years ago. Apparent slow punctures were in fact caused by badly internally corroded and hence porous rims. I found some replacement wheels eventually through contacts in the Lotus Clubs and had them fitted and balanced to my satisfaction. The chap who I bought them from had a large collection of wheels in an attempt to find as near perfect a set of wheels as he could find. He was in fact putting the finishing touches to an Elan +2, which intended for high-speed autobahn work in Germany.

Chapter 12

FITTING THE BODY

This is relatively straight forward as it is practically a reversal of the dismounting procedure. Much more care should be exercised, as you would not want any damage to occur to it at this stage. This is done in two stages, one to mark out the fixing holes in the chassis, and the final fitting when the holes have been drilled and tapped.

Glue down the felt to the chassis backbone, not forgetting to cut the holes for the front propshaft access

Body of the Sprint just mounted on the completed rolling chassis

and the seat belt anchors. Then with your army of helpers, lift the body sufficiently to clear the engine and rear uprights, and lower down gently onto the chassis. The body will attempt to find its own location guided by the rear chassis tubes and the interference of the felt. With your band of lifters taking the weight of the body, make sure that the body is as far forward as it will go to ensure that the body bobbins in front of the parcel shelf are in contact with the chassis. If you fail to do this, the body will be stressed in these areas and could cause localised cracking.

Bounce the body up and down a few times onto the chassis to ensure it is as far down as it can be. After doing this, have a good look around the mounting points to ensure that the chassis reinforcing points are in line with the body bobbins. Look also at the front suspension damper upper mountings to make sure these are clear of the body or, if holes already exist, that they are in the right position. Then place the bonnet into position making sure that it has at least $^{1}/_{4}$ in clearance from the camcover.

At this point you will probably find that some of the body mounting points are not touching the chassis. This is normal due to manufacturing tolerances and the gaps should be made up with large penny washers. These washers may also have to be added to ensure clearance of the cam cover.

When you are finally happy with the body position, mark out the holes with a felt tip pen or spray paint down the fixing holes. If the hole is a tapped one in the body, clear out all traces of paint before attempting to fit a bolt. Referring to the workshop manual at this stage, check that you have marked out every hole including the ones that reside behind the dashboard. I have heard horror stories of these holes being missed and they are virtually impossible to drill and tap with the heater and dashboard in position.

Remove the body, carefully, and place back onto the railway sleepers.

Carefully ascertain the centre of each of the holes and indent with a centre punch and hammer. Precision at this point will save a lot of fiddling later. Drill each of the holes with a 4 or 5mm pilot drill ensuring that the holes are square to their relative faces. Drill out to the correct tapping drill size at the tapped hole positions. Drill with the correct clearance drill size at the threaded hole positions in the body. Tap the holes as required in the chassis, using copious amounts of oil as a lubricant. The last thing you need in your chassis is a broken tap. Clear away all swarf and debris from the chassis and have a good clear up. A

The body back on the new chassis. Where's the beer?

body will not fit correctly on bits of metal and the odd drill left lying around. After drilling and tapping holes, fit the body straightaway. Bodies of GRP can move when stored on anything else but a chassis.

Position the body back on the chassis as before and bolt up, not forgetting the cross brace at the back between the suspension towers.

Chapter 13

ELECTRICS

Heater
Replace the baby Elan heater intake plenum chamber if it has been removed. Ensure that the drain hose at the bottom is intact and mates up with the hole in the body and is adequately sealed with silicone sealant. Pour water into the plenum to test this feature or the carpets will never be dry. Before fitting the plenum chamber, fit any soundproofing that you may have removed against the engine bulkhead.

The heater unit on the baby Elan is a simple affair that is easily stripped down. Clean it out and pressure test to make sure there are no water leaks. Test the fan motor for quiet operation on both speeds. Rectifying faults like these at this stage are much easier than finding them in a fully assembled car. The same applies to the +2 heater but this is a little more complex. Connect the heater pipes to the heater unit

ensuring the pipe runs do not interfere with other dashboard fitted items, such as the radio on the baby Elan. The +2 heater pipe connections are made on the engine side of the bulkhead and are just as inaccessible when the carburettors are in place.

Wiper motor, mechanisms and washer jets
Inspect, clean, lubricate and test all the moving parts, replacing any suspect or broken items. These are again almost impossible to access with the dashboard in place. Assemble in accordance with the workshop manual and fit the washer jets with their associated plumbing. Test the wiper mechanism action by connecting to a 12-volt power source.

The Dashboard
Fitting a new dashboard to an Elan is not easy. This is when your photographs, notes and diagrams at the

A Sprint dashboard in non standard Walnut veneer

The same Walnut dash from the passenger side

A standard Sprint straight grain dash minus radio

strip down stage will prove invaluable. If you are to use the old loom, you will have labelled each of the wires as to where they came from. On older Elans it was fashionable at the time to add extra switches, gauges and dials so your old loom may be a bit of a mystery. Wires may be missing, cut out for some obscure reason and additions made just to confuse. If you are happy with the old loom and have tested every circuit to ensure continuity and checked every terminal and all the bindings, then reuse it by all means but bear in mind that old looms age and crack just like we do.

If the dashboard is badly disfigured by previous owners over enthusiasm or just by the ravishes of time then a new dash is recommended, straight grain for a baby Elan and burred walnut for a +2. Some baby Elan restorers are attracted to burred walnut but it was never fitted at the factory as standard.

Know Your Limits - Disaster Awaits

If you are not at all happy with the state of the existing loom, take it out and put on one side. Do not throw it away at this stage, as you will learn later. With a new loom at least you know that it has new wire in it, built with all new connectors and bound up to ensure that the cables come out of the loom where

they should, and not dangling dangerously like spaghetti.

Old looms can cause all sorts of problems, from high resistance to cable faults, wire breakage at points where you cannot get at them and, worst of all, electrical fires. High currents through high resistance cables causes heat, heat causes fires. An electrical fire in a steel-bodied car is bad enough, in a GRP car it could be catastrophic.

When I first bought my Elan +2, the wiring was awful. I had 18 volts coming out of the dynamo regulator and only 8 volts at the headlamps. The regulator had been re-adjusted in an attempt to give some illumination but on numerous occasions the voltage would fluctuate so much it blew headlight bulbs all the time. I eventually removed the volt losses by remaking all the connections, fitting a ring main earthing system and ensuring the loom was in a serviceable condition. I eventually fitted an alternator to power the heated rear screen I had fitted, and also quartz halogen headlights to improve upon the standard Elan, meagre, night time candlepower.

If you feel you are not up to this, for piece of mind, buy a new loom.

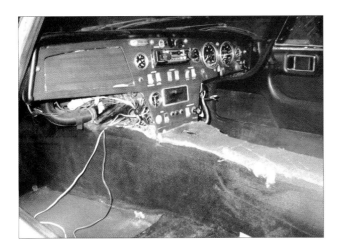

The Sprint dashboard prior to restoration. Extra dials, light and switches added by previous owners. Veneer was suffering too

Dashboard after restoration. Totally standard. Note the three sub looms waiting to be connected up after individual testing

My Sprint's dashboard rear on removal

The Wiring Diagram

The easiest way to read a wiring diagram from the workshop manual is to have it enlarged. Your local art print shop will do this for you at a modest cost. A1

Rear of dashboard – after. Note the tank tape around the glove box. This holds the cables in place for the ignition isolation switch and left hand window motor

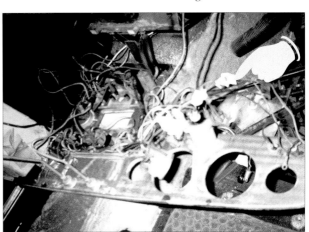

Rear of dashboard – before. The white tags on each cable identify them as they are removed

size is good to read but you could have two A2 blowups, one of each half and then stick them together. Most of the diagram is reasonably easy to follow as long as you follow the colour coding for each circuit. There is a small anomaly here in that some loom manufacturers use the new international colour coding system that does have slight variances over the old system. You will find these as they appear so do not be surprised when some wires appear odd colours.

If you did not make a record of switch terminations, or if the loom is in a bad state of repair behind the dashboard, particularly on the S4 and Sprint models, the wiring diagram will not show you which termination to use for each cable. For those of you who find yourselves in this position I have included,

The finished dashboard

just for you, a diagram I made up for my Sprint in the Appendices.

Rewire

The wiring loom will normally be in three sections, the dashboard, the engine bay and the interior. The interior section also includes the boot wiring.

All three sections join together behind the dashboard with bullet connectors. This will be a tight squeeze so be extra careful on cable routing. The +2 and baby Elan cable routings follow different paths mainly due to the heater configuration. Your new loom may not be an exact replica of the original so you have to figure out the optimum cable run that the loom designer used in its manufacture.

Start with the dashboard laid face down on the bench on a cloth to prevent scratching the polished veneer. With all instruments and switches in position, except for the water temperature/oil pressure combined gauge in the baby Elan, lay out the dash section of the loom over the instruments and identify from your wiring diagram which cable goes where. A logic will

begin to appear as each cable in turn exits from the loom at the required position. You may need a number of attempts at getting the loom orientation correct, but with a little patience it will all unfold.

The +2 loom enters from below the heater, the baby Elan's from above. In both cases, space is at a premium, particularly between the rear of the dash and the heater casing on the latter. On the old loom installation, there should have been a number of P clips that located the loom at various positions behind the dash. Use these clips, or preferably new ones, in the same manner, routing the main cable harness between switches and instruments in a neat and tidy manner. The actual route will depend on the design of the harness that should become apparent as you thread it through the maze of switches and instruments.

The principle aim is to install the loom behind the dash in such a manner that cables do not rub against each other or chafe against surrounding objects, such as the heater casing. The heater casing is grounded to earth, so any short circuit you get in this area could be terminal. Use additional P clips to ensure that the loom stays in position. The other aim is to be able to install the dash into the car with all cables connected in such a manner that the dash can be laid down on its face in the car for testing purposes.

Remember that earlier you were advised not to throw the old loom away just yet. It serves a number of purposes. If it was marked up as I advised, you can identify any changes made to the colour of the cables. It could give some reminder as to how it was initially fed, and finally, it gives a source of cable colours that could prove otherwise hard to get hold of. This last point is important to the Series 4 Elan and Sprint where you could find supplementary earth

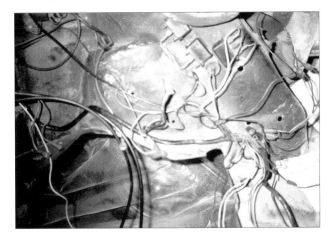

Under bonnet electrics – before. Rough

cable missing for the window motor switches. The basic loom does not include wiring for the electric radiator fan and Otter switch either so having a surplus of cable is handy at any time, which enables you to follow the correct colour codes.

Lay out the engine bay harness, with the lighting and ignition circuits, in the front well of the body. Connect cables to the generator and the fuse box. If the car has a dynamo, connect all Lucar connections to the control box. Feed the main harness through the bulkhead ensuring the grommet makes a good seal using a silicone sealant, as you should with all the other bulkhead penetrations. Connect the cables to the lighting, flashing and horn relays and feed the remainder of the cables to headlights, sidelights, flashers, repeaters, if fitted, and finally to the ignition coil.

When the engine bay loom has been routed, neatly position and form to follow the inner wing profile and

then hold down with P clips. At this stage check all of the circuits with a multi-meter, or a battery and 12-volt bulb, before connecting to the dashboard loom. Start testing at each of the lighting circuits to ensure all earths are functioning, and that each item powers up, or lights up, on application of battery power. This procedure will eliminate any faults at their source and will make them easier to locate and rectify rather than waiting until the entire loom is connected up.

After testing, neatly route the cables in the body nose, and hold in place with cable ties, so that the bullet connectors are kept off the nose floor. Route

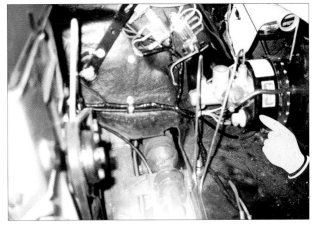

Under bonnet electrics – after. Note the new Girling servo unit in position

the lighting cables, especially the headlight cables, so that the action of the headlight pop-up mechanisms does not interfere with the cables. This makes for a much neater installation than the usual 'ball of tangled string' and keeps bullet connectors out of pools of water. This is a common electrical problem with Elan headlights caused by badly corroded bullet connections.

Follow the previous procedure for the cabin loom feeding the main cable down the nearside sill on the baby Elan, and under the sill carpet on the +2.

In order to prevent corrosion of all connections smear them with petroleum jelly, making sure that all bullet connections are firmly pushed into their sleeves the full length. Connect all the bullets on the three sub looms as per the wiring diagram. Test all the circuits with the battery connected with an ammeter in the circuit. Flash the battery earth lead first to make sure there is not a dead short anywhere. Test each circuit in turn and note the ammeter reading to ensure that excess current is not being drawn. A more likely fault will be a bad earth connection that should be rectified before final assembly.

A common fault on all Elans is the isolation switch in the glove box. Many owners in the past have diverted the wiring around this switch thereby making this feature ineffective. The switch can be disassembled, cleaned and made to work, but requires a little patience and dexterity.

Once you are happy with all the wiring, feed the loom excess cabling over the plenum on the baby Elan, and down the left-hand side of the heater space on the +2. At the same time position the dashboard, keeping a close eye on any loose cables and particularly the main dash loom bundle as it occupies the space between the dash and the heater casing. Push the dashboard into position and fix in place with the chromed, cross-headed screws complete with fibre washers. Connect all the remaining minor connections such as courtesy light switches, window winder motors and retest everything.

The battery earth lead is connected to one of the chassis bolts in the boot. Rear lighting earths also use the same point. Ensure the bobbin in the body is clean and free from corrosion. Smear the bobbin and earth lead termination with petroleum jelly. Ensure the nut is tight by holding the body bolt head with a spanner to prevent it from turning and tightening the nut with a socket to the recommended torque quoted in the workshop manual.

Corrosion and loose connections at any earthing point have caused many a Lotus owner problems, me included. I have added supplementary earths on both my +2 and Sprint to avoid this.

I have gone into more detail on this subject than any other part of the rebuild. This is for the simple reason that more Elans have been written off due to electrical fires than have been caused by any other single reason. This could be attributed to amateurish modifications to the cars electrical system rather than the original factory build. Do not let yours be one of them.

Chapter 14

FINISHING THE BODY

Windows

The +2 door window motors and mechanisms are a vast improvement on the baby Elan's flimsy wires and bobbins. They are almost un-burstable and should give very little trouble in service. A good cleaning and greasing of the mechanism runner at the bottom of the window is usually all that is required. Follow the workshop manual to the letter if you are going to dismantle the doors and winder mechanisms. This, of course, goes for the baby Elan, but you will probably have to anyway.

The lower section of the baby Elan's window frames can badly corrode whereby the wire guide pulleys

Decrepit window frame. The bottom section is steel, the rest is brass. The lower section was replaced and then the whole lot rechromed

Window winder capstan wheel prior to renovation

will seize up, wearing prematurely. The whole lower frame could collapse rendering the motor useless. These frames can be replaced at a high cost. An alternative is to have the lower steel section replaced with a new piece and then the whole frame re-chromed.

Re-fitting the wires and pulleys can be a difficult job. Follow the workshop manual to the letter. Tension-

ing the cables and tightening up the pinch bolts can be a frightening experience, especially if the window breaks. They can go with quite a bang, usually after they have been tightened. If the cable pinch bolt nuts are not tight enough, the cable will slip through and fall off the capstan pulley. A simple nip is all that is required, just sufficient to deform the cable. An extra cable-securing tip is to add a little soft solder on the cables just as they leave the pinch bolt. Do not drop hot solder onto the glass though unless you like big bangs.

Trim

If you are lucky, the trim could be serviceable with a good clean. If the car has not been abused inside they can wear quite well. If a smoker has dropped cigarette ends onto vinyl coverings or sharp objects have ripped the seats then a re-trim could be called for. Seat trim kits are available, but the ribbed, textured pattern used on later models, and +2, is difficult to source. Many trimmers with a good sewing machine can reproduce this affect with good quality stitching.

All Elan seats suffer from padding ageing and com-

My Sprint interior prior to restoration

The interior of the Sprint was in good condition apart from the dashboard

pression. The rubber mattress webbing on +2S seats can split and rot. These can be repaired with standard webbing and new foam cut to shape by hand. Stitching and assembly of the later +2 seats is best left to the professional trimmer.

Head linings can be cleaned if soiled. Some original patterns, particularly the +2 diamond pattern, are difficult to source.

Carpet sets can be obtained cheaply enough and are not difficult to fit.

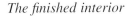

The finished interior

Chapter 15

THE BOOT

Petrol tank

The +2 petrol tank is neatly positioned behind the rear seats, between the rear suspension turrets. As such it is saved from most of the corrosion problems of the baby Elan's position in the bottom of the boot.

Remove the tank and inspect for any leakage. Small holes can be repaired if the tank is adequately steam cleaned internally to remove all traces of petrol vapour. If the tank is badly corroded, get a replacement. Remove all traces of rust and paint. When the paint is dry and hard, rust proof the under side with rust proofing wax.

Because of its higher position the +2 tank feed pipe is half way down the tank. To enable it to be filled

The Sprint petrol tank removed from the boot, finished in new black paint

Petrol tank back in the boot. Just enough room for the spare wheel. Note the new wiring to the light clusters. Finishing backboard is yet to be attached to the brackets

to the top it has a complex breather system comprising of two plastic pipes being fed from the top corners of the tank. These breather pipes run upwards over the roof lining, crossing each other in the process, down the other side, alongside the rear vent, and then through the rear inner sill to emerge under the car.

If these breathers are allowed to chafe against the bodywork in the vent area they will eventually wear through. If the connection is not secure on the tank they will leak for the same reason. All +2 breathers emit petrol vapour under the car. That is how they work. If there is a strong smell of petrol in the boot, check these breather pipes. Adversely, if the breather pipes block, you will not be able to fill the tank.

Petrol gauge sender unit

While you have the petrol tank out of the car, check the petrol gauge sender unit. You should be able to hear the float moving if you shake the tank about. Put a multi-meter across the terminals and check for change in resistance as the tank is tilted. If in doubt, replace the sender unit now while it is easy to get at.

Boot locking mechanism

The boot lock on the baby Elan, and early +2, is a simple latch directly coupled to an external handle. Later +2s have a remote device connected to a pull handle in the driver's door opening. If the cable breaks it will be necessary to take out the rear seats, the left-hand rear trim and the rear sill closure plate in order to gain access to the Bowden cable sleeve nut. Not the easiest of jobs, but if a +2 has not had its original sill closure plates replaced by now they will have corroded away a long time ago. Now is the time to replace them.

Chapter 16

SILL MEMBERS

In order to accommodate the longer body length of the +2, and give some additional sideways protection, steel structural members are bolted to the inner sill between the inner and the outer sills. The lower outer sill seam is bolted through the sill member to the inner sill, which provides for vastly improved stiffness. The centre reinforcing plates also act as anchor points for the seat belts. At each end of the sill members are tubes welded into the structure to serve as jacking points.

If a +2 has not had the original sill members replaced

My +2 sill members after I had replaced them. Note the abundance of Wax oil.

they are probably lying in heaps at the bottom of the sills. Having taken the sill rear closure plate off to gain access to the boot release cable, have a good look at the sill member. If it is still covered in paint and rust proofing wax, and more so is all there, then you are lucky. Someone has already done it. If it is just a mass of rusty bits resembling nothing at all, covered in road filth, then you will need new ones. Complete kits are available from various sources that include reinforcing plates, sill closure plates and all fixings.

This job is easiest to do when the body is off the chassis, resting on the railway sleepers. This gives good access without the suspension and hubs getting in the way. With all seats and carpets removed note where the three reinforcing plates are positioned on each side. There are one at the front and back and one in the middle. These will probably be badly corroded, as will be all the nuts and bolts.

Wire brush as much of the dirt and rust off the nuts and bolts as you can, then apply penetrating fluid to all the fixings and leave for 24 hours. Some of the bolt heads will snap off being so badly corroded. Some may unscrew if you are lucky, the remainder will require an angle grinder or electric drill. It is not an easy job.

When all the fixings have been removed including the ones in the bottom seams, carefully prise the outer sill away from the inner sill at the bottom

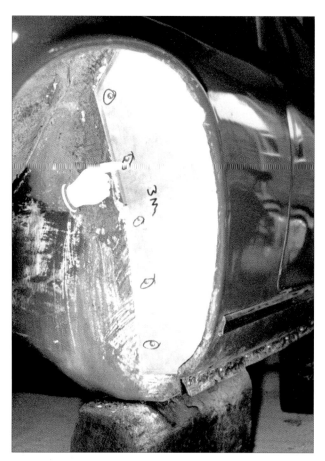

Stainless steel sill closing plate bolted into position with stainless steel nuts and screws

seam. It will come apart eventually but be careful not to damage the GRP in doing so. Pull the remains of the sill member out from the rear, sweep up onto a shovel and dispose. Just like I did. Remove the inner reinforcing plates and dispose. Clean everything out and make any necessary repairs to the sill GRP as required.

Replacement mild-steel sill members are often galvanised, if not give a good coat of paint, primer and topcoat. In both cases, give a liberal coating of rust proofing wax. The same treatment should be given to the reinforcing plates.

Prise open the sills again and feed in at the rear the new sill members, sandwiched between the inner and outer sill at the lower seam. Position the reinforcing plates, the one containing the seat belt tapped boss is in the middle, and bolt up. Drill holes for the bottom seam fixings through the new sill member then bolt up with new nut and bolts. If you can get hold of stainless steel nuts and bolts all the better, just in case you have to do the job again.

You can now be reassured that your seat belts will hold you in, and if you ever have to use the side jack, it will not disappear into the body or worse still, collapse while you have the wheel off at the side of the road.

Chapter 17

UNDER THE BONNET

Hydraulics

In most cases old vehicles hydraulic systems will be suspect, with seals and cylinder bores all in need of replacement. If they all look as if they have not been renewed lately, then replace with new, including a new servo unit if one was fitted originally.

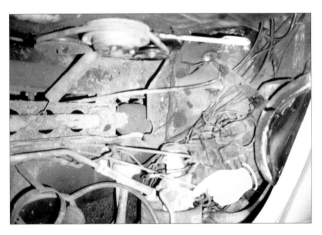

Pre-restoration electrics. Every thing was binned including the servo that was returned to manufacturers on acquisition of a replacement

Under bonnet nose – after. Note the copper brake pipes (1). The heavy earth lead (2) connected to the chassis bobbin runs direct to the battery in parallel with the feed. One of my subtle mods

Early view of nose cone prior to restoration

Under bonnet nose – before. Rust galore

New brake and clutch master cylinders in position, all piped up. Note the stainless steel braided flexible hose on the clutch master cylinder

Original Girling Power Stop servo units are getting difficult to find as they are only available part exchange. They do turn up at brake specialists from time to time, if they get old ones back. So remember to return yours, another enthusiast may be dependent on you. Lockheed units can be made to fit but in slightly revised positions.

Fit all new hydraulic hoses in the engine compartment, and all new flexible hoses, preferably stainless steel braided, on the brakes and clutch slave cylinders. Fill the systems with Dot 4 brake fluid and bleed to remove all entrapped air.

Carburettors

Weber, Dellorto or Stromberg, there is not a lot to choose between the three. Weber DCO40s are the traditional fitment, with Dellorto filling gaps in when Weber could not supply for whatever reason. Strombergs were Lotus' attempt at meeting emissions regulations and, without the re-circulation idler

Engine all ready to go. The original Weber DCO 40's came up beautifully

JVV 200G in full working trim. Kept clean like this it was very reliable. Note the stainless steel braided flexible hose on the clutch master cylinder

mixture system installed for the North American market, could be made to work just as efficiently as the 4-branch systems.

Whatever system is fitted to your car, it will not function correctly if it has been neglected and left in a bad state of repair. When the carburettors are removed at stripdown stage, check first of all that the Thackery double coil washers have not been tightened up completely. If they have, check that the O rings have not been extruded from their carriers, if they have the carriers could be split. The usual damage due to overtightening of carburettor nuts, and this is common to most vehicles, not just Lotus, is that the carburettor flanges will be distorted. This condition will lead to air leakage into the system, weak mixtures and all the accompanying complaints that go with it. Least of all, the car will never run correctly. Distort-

A concours winning early Elan +2 on Stromberg carbs

The +2 engine bay during its first restoration

My Sprint's engine bay prior to fitting carbs and ancillaries

Phil Gaskell's Sprint's engine bay

A concourse Sprint engine bay

A Sprint engine bay, exhaust side. Note the new windscreen washer bag

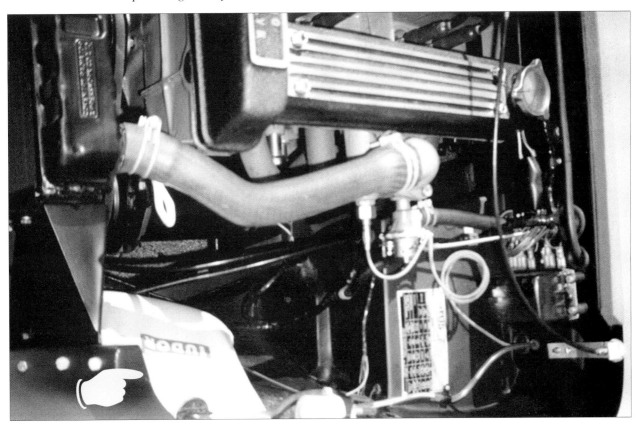

The same engine bay. Note the plastic electric radiator fan. Lotus used what they could get hold of at the time

My Sprint's nose cone. The original metal electric radiator fan was refitted after bead blasting and final powder coating

ed flanges can be flattened but it is a skilled job to get right. If they are really bad, the only recourse to take is the purchase of a new set of carburettors. Ouch!

Strip the carburettors as per the workshop manual but stop at removing the butterflies and spindles. If they are badly damaged, or too stiff to operate properly, seek advice from a carburettor specialist. Clean the

units inside and out with petrol and a stiff brush. Examine all the jets for blockages and that they are all the correct size as per the workshop manual. Carburettor cleaning agents in aerosols can be purchased from most motor factors, which will transform the appearance of the old carburettors. Leave all the internal channels and passages to soak in this liquid, then blast through with compressed air to remove any

The same engine at bottom of previous page, from a different angle

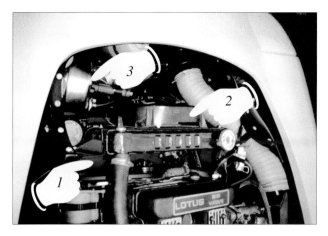

Phil Gaskell's Sprint's nose cone. Note the Spyder chassis (1), cowled electric fan (2) and Lockheed servo unit (3). All of Phil's mods have made this a very reliable car

Another view of Phil's Sprint's nose cone

ingress of foreign matter. Leave to dry then give all the external features a thorough clean with Solvol Autosol.

Refit all the jets, replace the float valves with new ones and reassemble the floats. Always check the float heights with the workshop manual. Incorrect float heights will give incorrect petrol/air mixtures that will lead to all kinds of running problems. Replace all gaskets and seals and finish reassembling the carburettors.

Assemble the carburettors onto the engine with new O rings in the carriers and tighten the nuts so that the Thackery washers have a remaining 1mm gap. Fit a new braided fuel pipe from the fuel pump to the carburettors with new fibre washers on the banjo bolts. For extra security, a good after market extra is the aero standard swivel hoses, which dispense with the banjo couplings. Banjo bolts have been known to shake loose leading to nasty petrol leaks over the distributor, especially if the fibre washers are not replaced every time you take them off.

Fit the carburettor back plate, trumpets, air box, intake hose and air filter housing in the nose cone.

Radiator

Water-cooling radiators on Elans come in all shapes and sizes. The early Elans were unique to Lotus, then a Standard Triumph unit was adapted. This was a full width unit that was just about up to the job if kept in good fettle. Later models used narrower units

that made the cooling even more marginal. On the S4, Sprint and +2S130 models, Lotus fitted blanking plates under and around the radiator in an attempt to encourage all the air entering the front grill to pass though the radiator.

The engine-mounted radiator-cooling fan was of little use in traffic jams, so Lotus resorted to an electric cooling fan. This functions reasonably well with the radiator mounted Otter switch, but only on well-cleaned radiators and engine water passages. If you intend to retain the original two-core radiator, back flush it out with a water hose directed into the bottom pipe until the water comes out clean from the top pipe. When the engine is finally running, use a proprietary flushing agent, which will remove any build up of lime scale that detracts from good heat transfer.

A better solution is to upgrade the radiator to a three core modern matrix that allows for much better cooling in high ambient temperatures and use of the engine performance potential. Most radiator specialists are capable of doing this work utilising the existing radiator top and bottom head tanks. Complete with the existing side plates, they do not detract from the original appearance but will give greater assurance that water temperature is not going to be a problem. Modern pancake cooling fans can be fitted but are not necessary if the original is serviceable and you wish to retain the original look.

Fix in place the blanking plates and foam to the bonnet to ensure that cooling air does not escape round the radiator. On S4 and Sprints two holes are cut into the nearside inner wing covered in wire mesh.

Phil's Sprint nose cone from another angle

Ensure this mesh is clear as it allows air to circulate in what would otherwise be a very hot region, being directly over the exhaust manifold.

If you live in a hard water area, containing an abundance of lime, your kettle will tell you this, fill the radiator with rainwater. This may be difficult at certain times of the year so keep a stock. If you live in a soft water area, tap water will do. In both cases use a 50:50 solution of antifreeze to water all year round.

My Sprint's radiator showing mounting of the Otter switch which controls the electric fan

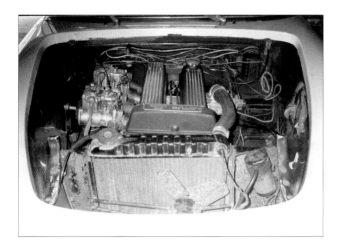 

Engine bay – before. Note that the engine is a little low on the left. The carbs were resting on the body because the left hand engine mount had collapsed

Engine bay – after.
A little time and patience is all it needs

Apart from frost protection, this will also give corrosion protection, essential for a twin cam head and as an added bonus increases the boiling temperature of the water.

It is sometimes difficult to ensure a complete fill of the cooling system, particularly the heater circuit. Make sure that the heater control is on hot and remove the heater pipe at the cylinder head until all the trapped air has been dispelled, then refit.

The Otter switch, or thermostatically controlled switch for the electric fan, is usually positioned in the radiator top header tank. It is simply pushed into a rubber grommet to seal and retain. This should be held in place by wire or preferably cable ties. It can be embarrassing if this blows out, makes a mess of the engine bay and paintwork, and not least, if you do not turn the engine off quickly, can ruin all your hard work.

Fit the expansion bottle bracket in its original position, either in the nose cone or behind the radiator. Fill the bottle with 1 inch of water/antifreeze mix and connect the hose to the radiator overflow pipe.

Chapter 18

PREPARATION FOR THE BIG DAY

Setting up

Fill the petrol tank and then raise the car to sit on railway sleepers on its wheels. Work the suspension to level out the ride height. Weight the car as recommended in the workshop manual or ask some nimble people of similar weight to sit in the car. With the torque wrench set at the correct readings, tighten up all the suspension nuts and bolts that were left loose previously. Return the car to the ground and check the ride height with the heights quoted in the workshop manual.

Before you do anything else, check all around the car for the obvious things you may have missed. Double check that all hoses are tight and that there are no petrol leaks. Connect up the battery and remove the

Under the bonnet. All finished and ready to fire up

Custard on the sea front at Blackpool. A magazine shot, courtesy of David Bowers

spark plugs from the engine. Turn the engine by hand with a spanner on the engine pulley bolt, ensuring that all is free. Remove the spanner.

Turn the engine on the starter motor for about 30 seconds and check the oil pressure gauge responds. Check the static ignition timing with a 12-volt bulb and readjust as required to the setting for your particular car quoted in the workshop manual.

With a spark plug on number 1 lead, check for a spark with the ignition on and engine turning on the starter motor. If all is correct, insert the spark plugs after adding a little copper grease to the threads on the plugs.

Shots of Custard at final stages of build

Me and Custard. Another magazine shot, courtesy of David Bowers

Me and Custard. A magazine shot, courtesy of David Bowers

If you have not done already, screw in the slow running mixture screws gently until they bottom, then unscrew two turns.

Fire up
With Weber carburettors, jab the throttle a couple of times, with Dellortos and Strombergs pull out the choke. Turn the key and start the engine. If you are lucky it will probably start first time but will run a little lumpy. Do not rev the engine but keep it on a light throttle until the engine gets warm. When warm it should smooth out a little but may not tick over properly. Increase the slow running tick-over screw on the carburettor until the engine ticks over smoothly, preferably below 1,000rpm.

Have another look around the engine for water, oil or petrol leaks. Tighten up hoses as required. Switch off the engine.

Tune Up
Check the ignition with a strobe light at tick-over and adjust as required. Increase the engine revs slowly and observe that the ignition advance is operating correctly as per the workshop manual.

The workshop manual method of setting the slow running mixtures is satisfactory when you have had sufficient practice. For the inexperienced I would recommend that you buy, or borrow, a carburettor air flow meter and a colour tune. Synchronise the two carburettors by adjusting the balance screw so that the airflow down each choke is equal. This can also be done with a length of hose in the ear and the other end close to a carburettor trumpet. Equal sounds mean equal airflow. That is the theory and it can work for the experienced ear. After synchronisation, the idle speed may require further adjustment.

At this stage the idle mixture can be set for each choke in turn. Remove the plugs from 1 and 2 cylinders and replace with two colour tunes. One at a time will do but it is quicker with two. Start the engine and turn the screws in to weaken the mixture and out to richen. When you have a Bunsen blue flame (Royal Blue) turn the screw in further until there is

Custard from a different angle courtesy of David Bowers

no flame at all. You will notice at this moment a change in engine note and a slight drop in revs. This is the situation that the workshop manual is describing, but if you have never done this before you would not know what you were listening for. Turn the idling screw out slowly until the Bunsen blue flame reappears. The engine revs will increase slightly and the engine should run more smoothly. Repeat this procedure for each cylinder in turn. As you finish tuning number 4 cylinder, you will find the engine runs pretty smooth and you become an expert overnight.

During all the setting up and tuning operations, keep an eye on the water temperature gauge to check the temperature does not exceed 90 deg C.

For overall fine-tuning of the car's systems, a rolling road is necessary in order to make adjustments at various engine speeds under variable load conditions. The factory settings will be satisfactory for most of us but if optimum performance is required for competition use then a rolling road tune-up will be necessary. After the final tune-up check again for any oil and water leaks and correct as necessary.

With your insurance sorted, take the car to your local MOT station and watch the testers chin hit the floor.

Running in
Do not exceed more than 3,000rpm in any gear for the first 1,000 miles.

Do not allow the engine to labour in high gear, particularly going up steep hills.

Increase revs gradually for the next 1,000 miles. After this do not exceed 5,000rpm for another 1,000 miles.

If the engine has a tendency to run over 90 deg C at these speeds, check it out carefully.

If the engine behaves over all this period of reserved running in it will pay dividends in long-term, trouble-free running. Remember, keep the revs below 5,000rpm and keep the rest in reserve for short bursts. That is the bit that GTi owners hate.

Change engine oil and filter.
Repeat tune-up procedure to check nothing has moved, adjust as required.

Enjoy

Chapter 19

PREPARING ELANS FOR CONCOURS PRESENTATION

There are two ways of starting off with a classic car of any description for concours presentation. One is to be extremely fortunate in having a totally original low mileage example that has never been out in the wet and treated with TLC since it left the factory. The second is to rebuild a well-used or neglected example to a standard equal to the first.

The first option is extremely difficult to realise because of the rarity of such finds, and if you did, they command such a high price they become like a collectors wine were the cork is never removed from the bottle.

Since the second option is the most likely contender, it is imperative that the standard of the build and finish is as good as or approaching that of the factories.

When renovation is undertaken, adhere to the standard specification wherever possible and avoid bolt on goodies even if they were a period fitting. If you are to use the car on a regular basis then hidden improvements cannot be frowned upon such as fitting an alternator if later models of the same car had them fitted at the factory. The same goes for tyres as long as they are a modern equivalent.

The main pointers in restoring an Elan for concours is that the body must be resprayed off the chassis with everything removed. If the fitting of a new chassis is part of the renovation process then all the better. This ensures that all edges, shut lines and profiles are finished off without impedance from adjoining items and fittings. Most of all it is over-spray which spoils most car body resprays. While the body is totally naked, the engine compartment, boot, nose-

Full frontal. Clean lines with registration letters on front grill

Rear quarter

Above Note door shutlines. Attention to detail at body shop is essential. Door bottoms never did fit flush even when new.

Nearside headlight pod in down position. Smooth profiles

Original Lucas headlight relays. Relays are clear laquered to prevent corrosion.

Under bonnet shot - note wiring with 'P' clips to hold cables in position

cone and wheel arches can all be attended to. Satin black is the best for these areas as it is easy to keep clean and less obvious than a gloss finish. Standard of finish under the bonnet should give a presentable surface that is easy to maintain, well flatted with no obvious damage marks.

The condition of a wiring loom throughout the car, particularly the engine compartment is all-important. If it is old and frayed with brittle discoloured insulation it can never contribute to the overall looks of the car. The only recourse is to renew the loom throughout. Installation should be neat and tidy with cable runs as per the original. Use of plastic P clips should

be as it left the factory and will be a compliment to the rest of the car. Wiring to the headlights, sidelights, direction indicators and relays should be especially neatly run, supported by 'P' clips and cable ties.

The most noticeable lump under the bonnet is of course the engine and here attention to detail can add to the overall ambience of the car. Essentially the engine should be oil-tight; not an easy feat with a Ford-Lotus Twin Cam but it can be done. Avoid over abundance of gasket sealant, which looks unsightly. As before, general overall finish of the engine counts a lot. Again colour should be as original. Some Lotus specialists know the formulae; Massey grey with a

Above   A clean and oil tight engine it can be achieved with patience

Left Engine compartment. Standard and spotless.

Clean alternator with tidy temperature gauge sender cable. All add to overall effect.

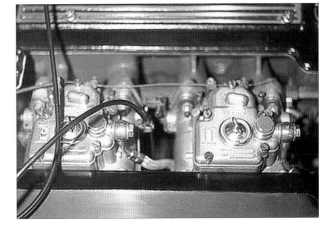

Weber DCO40's. Always keep clean.

tinge of green is the nearest that I can explain it. Cam covers should be finished as quoted in the manuals be it red, blue, green or black usually crackle finish paint all dependant on model. Twin Cam engines painted in all sorts of garish colours detract immensely.

Carburettors should be clean but not too highly polished. An even matt finish is desirable but difficult to keep clean over long periods. Hoses and clips should all be replaced with new. The purist will opt for the original wire clips but worm drive pipe clips will suffice for most people. Nuts and bolts are a contentious issue for the ardent concours builder. The extremist will only use black unfinished nuts and bolts where originally fitted. This is OK for the purist but they will rust at the first sign of rain. Cadmium plated fas-

teners are the next best thing, will look the part and at further expense, stainless steel can be used. Do not be tempted to chrome plate items that were never chromed on the original, they may look well in your eyes but will really get up the noses of real enthusiasts. All other under bonnet ancillaries should be painted gloss black.

Bright work on the rest of the car should look as good as you can afford. Rear boot hinges are relatively cheap to replace, as is the petrol filler cap. Rear light chrome rim backplates are a bit more expensive and are difficult to re-chrome. If yours are well past their best, used examples in good condition can be obtained for about half the price of new ones. Door window frames can be renovated and re-chromed; new ones are quite expensive.

Above World Championship Car Constructors badge

Right Erect headlight pod and finishing strip on front bumper. Original chrome work should be protected with wax polish

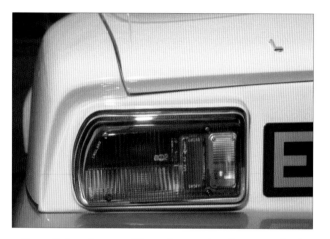

Rear light cluster. Clean internal reflectors which can get dirty and clean chrome surround to avoid corrosion. New chrome back plates are expensive but second-hand ones are available

Chrome locking petrol filler cap and boot hinges. Replacements are not expensive

L O T U S lettering on boot-lid and number plate lights can tarnish. New ones are readily available and can be easily fitted

Door handles can be rechromed. Door locks can be replaced with new ones

Above Window frames are expensive to replace. They can be refurbished and protected with wax polish. Correct filler strip for front screen rubber is hard to source.

Left Ventilator grill can be rechromed. New ones are expensive. Note original wire wiperblades.

Rear wheel. Powder coated and lacquered with rechromed spinners and new chrome embellishers.

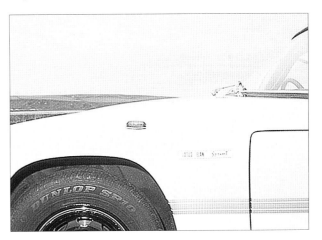

Above Elan Sprint badge and indicator repeaters add the finishing touches.

Left Quarter light extractor vent should be kept clean at all times

Wheels and tyres must look good and the only way is to start with undamaged rims. Dents should be repaired and if badly bent and bashed, replacement is the only way. Second hand wheels can be obtained but care is necessary to get true running ones. Have them bead blasted and finished in the system of your choice. Two-pack paint systems or powder coat is acceptable. Silver or black depends on the model. No other colour schemes were standard. Tyres as mentioned previously should be as close to the original as possible. Period tread patterns are available from specialists at a premium price but tyres of this size are readily available from most manufacturers. The slighter lower aspect ratios may upset the

For best results clean wheels inside and out off the car

Front-wheels - kept clean and polished they will always look good, avoid hitting with spinner mallet.

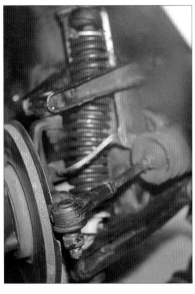

Left Front suspension, note braided hydraulic brake pipe for safety

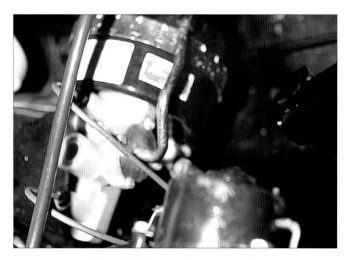

New Girling brake servo unit. Note the copper brake pipes.

purists. Kept clean and free from curb rubbing they should look the part. For myself, I consider tyre blacking cheapens the overall effect.

Running gear, brakes, suspension, should be as per the original, black painted or powder coated A frames and front suspension arms. Calipers are originally dull cadmium plated but this discolours easily with heat and corrosion soon sets in. Heat resistant paint is available for this specific purpose and can be made to look the part. Again avoid multi-coloured paint schemes. They will only cheapen the overall effect. Braided flexible brake pipes are not to be frowned on as they are considered a desirable modern safety feature. For the same reason and longevity, copper/nickel brake pipes are the best option.

The boot, again finished in black should be carpeted as per the original and boot boards in situ with any

finishing board. Battery and its associated cabling should be as new looking as possible.

Under the boot, exhaust systems can be original mild steel with all the inherent corrosion problems, or stainless steel which for most can be fitted and for-

Battery, well clamped onto shelf in the boot. Note neat cabling

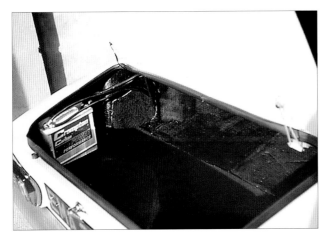

Black boot carpet, keep clean & tidy

Boot lid. Keep clean on the inside, avoid slamming down on tall suitcases!

Spare wheel is clamped to boot floor

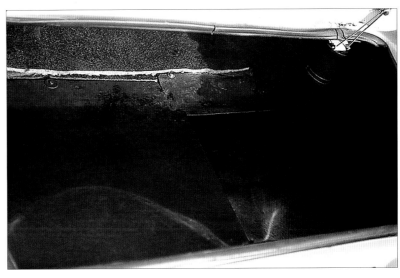

Boot board and petrol tank, all original and finished in black

gotten. Some makes don't make the right sounds, but most stainless systems stay looking good longer.

Last but not least, the car's interior. Apart from the exterior this is what most people will look at. Seats, door trim, centre console, headlining and carpeting should be as near to standard as possible. Seat trim kits are available at reasonable cost, as are carpet sets. Roof linings are harder to replace and should only be attempted with the front and rear screens removed.

Dashboards should be as standard but many Elans

Silencer. Tucked up neatly in boot floor recess.

Rear end. Nice and clean.

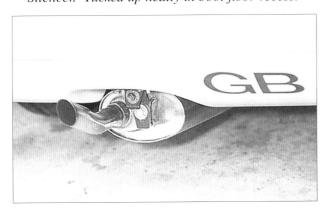

*Dashboard. Straight grain veneer standard
on all two seaters.*

*Door trim and locking mechanism
This is original but replacements are available*

*Drivers seat, keep clean with a damp cloth.
Retrim kits are available*

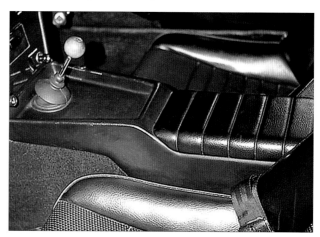

Centre console with correct gear lever gaitor rubber

Standard steering wheel with Colin Chapman's signature. Hard to replace and expensive.

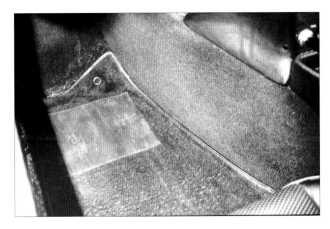

Passenger carpet. Bound edges and kept clean

Roof lining with interior light

had and even to this day can be bought new for extra gauges. Even burred walnut veneer can be obtained as an option, but if you are rebuilding your car with concours in mind, stick to the standard straight veneer.

Radios and CD players, what can I say about this one. If you fit an original Turn Lock radio, forget about ever listening to a pleasurable sound. All you will hear is engine crackle. Radio technology and suppression, especially on a fibreglass car was just not up to it. My car has a modern radio/cassette fitted

Proud owner at John o' Groats June 2001

with a removable front for security reasons. One day I will fit a period front piece just to look the part, then replace it with the modern front when I want to listen to it. The choice is yours but I like my music.

If you use your car regularly like I do then maintaining the standards previously outlined is a hurdle that can be overcome. I have often stated at Club Lotus meetings that the best way to maintain a car is to use it. Laying up of a car causes all sorts of problems with sticking and corrosion of moving parts and general maladies that affect unused vehicles. If you can store it in a humidity and temperature controlled environment then that is another matter, but the car will still require to be exercised at least once a month in the winter.

Maintenance is then more of a preventative nature than anything else. Waxoil all running gear including the chassis. Keep the body and brightwork clean at all times with a good coat of polish. In the winter months coat all the brightwork with lacquer or wax-oil. It can be easily removed with a cloth coated in white spirit.

Driving the car can make a world of difference to its overall looks. Keep a good distance from vehicles in front except of course for overtaking which should not take long any way. Avoid roads that have just been stone-chipped and if you cannot, drive reasonably slowly. In short do not attempt wheelies on gravel paths. That is a shortcut to disastrous body damage.

Finally, to keep a Lotus Elan in top running condition, use it, clean it regularly inside and out and maintain it to the book. In winter, keep it away from salted roads but exercise it when dry and conditions favourable.

Chapter 20

EPILOGUE

I am sure that you will appreciate this book for what it is. Many of the things I have written about I have tried to emulate. Not all of them, I must add, but I hope that many will learn from the mistakes I have made in the past.

I must at this stage, thank all the people I have come into contact with over the years who have helped me overcome countless problems with my two Elans. Personal friends I have made through Club Lotus and events I have attended. To the guys in the trade who have given me endless encouragement (remember what I said about future good customers). They know who they are. Last but not least, my wife Johanna, who has put up with a lot in the past. She did not like the time I spent in the garage, seemingly every night, to complete the +2 rebuild, but did not want me to sell it in the end. As for the Sprint rebuild

project, that was another matter.

The Elan Sprint has, since the completion of the restoration, been featured in a classic car magazine. It has won three concours events. But do not be deceived into thinking this car will be cosseted. It has already covered quite a few thousand miles, some of those thousands touring in central France. It has been exhibited at a number of Lotus events, and always driven there and back.

It has been a pleasure writing this volume as I thought to myself one day, 20 years of living with a Lotus must be capable of being written down to the benefit of others. If the two cars I saved from the big scrap heap in the sky are not enough, then passing on my experiences in this book is my way of saying, "Thank you Colin Chapman"

APPENDICES

Appendix i

BOOK LIST

Title	Author	Publisher
Lotus Elan - Official Workshop Manual*	Lotus Cars Limited	Lotus Cars Limited
Elan & +2 1962 - 1974	Paul Robinshaw and Christopher Ross	Motor Racing Publications
Lotus, The Elite, Elan, Europa	Chris Harvey	Oxford Illustrated Press
Lotus Elan. The Complete Story	Mike Taylor	Guild Publishing
Lotus Elan, Coupe, Convertible, Plus 2	Ian Ward	Osprey
Lotus Elan - Owners Workshop Manual*	Autobooks	Brooklands Books
Illustrated Lotus Buyers Guide	Graham Arnold	Motorbooks (Publishers Ltd)
Lotus. The Legend	David Hodges	Paragon
Lotus Elan Super Profile	Graham Arnold	Haynes
Lotus Elan Ultimate Portfolio 1962-1974	Compiled by R M Clarke	Brooklands Books
Lotus Elan & SE 1989-1992	Compiled by R M Clarke	Brooklands Books
Lotus Twin Cam Engine	Miles Wilkins	Osprey
Lotus. A Formula 1 Team History	Bruce Grant-Braham	The Crowood Press Ltd
The Illustrated Motorcar Legends - Lotus	Roy Bacon	Sunburst Books

* For further details of these books see page 106

ELAN S4 REAR DASH WIRING (LOOKING
FROM REAR OF DASH)

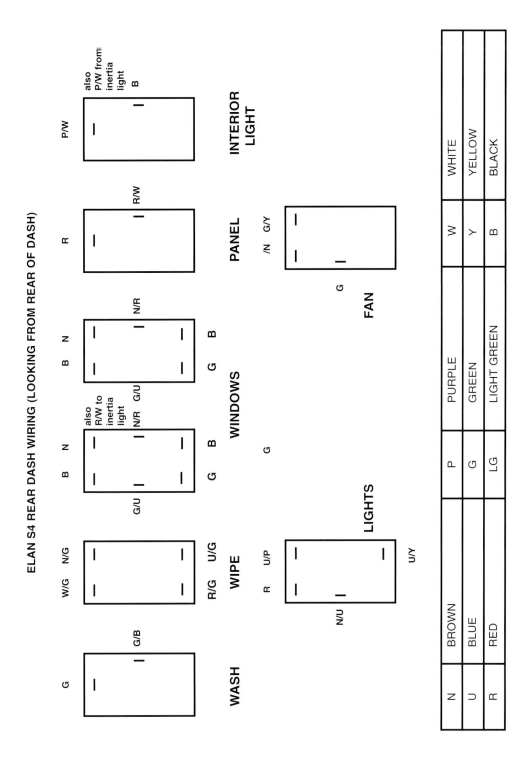

TECHNICAL DRAWINGS

Included here is a small selection of technical drawings taken from the Official Lotus Elan Workshop Manual and The Lotus Elan Owners Workshop Manual. They are included to give readers a better understanding of the mechanical side of the Elan. I would strongly recommend the purchase of one of these books before any serious rebuilding is undertaken.

Lotus Elan - Official Workshop Manual approx 250 pages, Part number X036T0327J. Available through any Lotus dealer or contact the Lotus Hot line: 08700 362277 or www.lotuscars.co.uk

Lotus Elan - Owners Workshop Manual 168 pages. Ref: OWM 600. Available from good bookshops or in case of difficulty from Brooklands Books Ltd. Tel: 01932 865051 e-mail: sales@brooklands-books.com or www.brooklands-books.com

All drawings and diagrams © Lotus Cars Limited 1964 and Brooklands Books 1981.

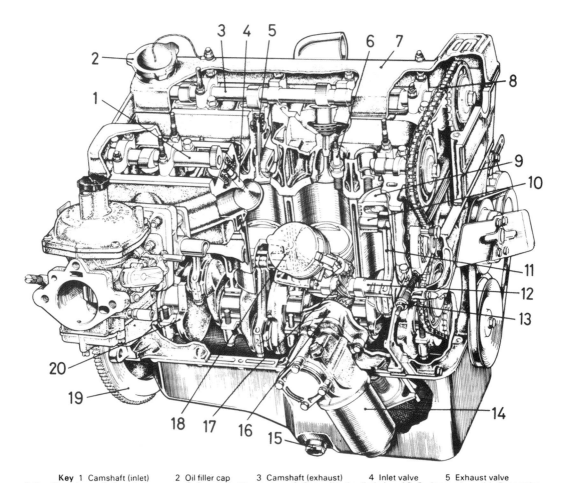

Key 1 Camshaft (inlet)   2 Oil filler cap   3 Camshaft (exhaust)   4 Inlet valve   5 Exhaust valve
6 Sparking plug   7 Camshaft cover   8 Camshaft drive chain   9 Piston (No 1 cylinder)   10 Gudgeon pin   11 Connecting
rod   12 Jackshaft   13 Camshaft drive chain tensioner   14 Oil filter   15 Sump drain plug   16 Oil pump   17 Jackshaft
skew gear (distributor and oil pump drive)   18 Distributor   19 Flywheel   20 Crankshaft

Cut-away view of the engine

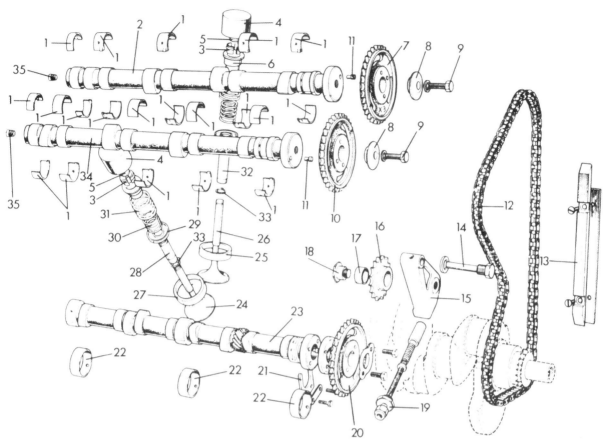

Key 1 Bearing shell (camshaft)   2 Camshaft (exhaust valves)   3 Split collets   4 Cam follower (tappet)
5 Adjusting shim   6 Spring seat (upper)   7 Camshaft sprocket (exhaust)   8 Washer   9 Bolt   10 Camshaft sprocket
(inlet)   11 Dowel   12 Camshaft drive chain   13 Chain slipper assembly   14 Tensioner bracket pivot bolt   15 Tensioner
bracket   16 Tensioner sprocket   17 Bush   18 Sprocket retainer   19 Tensioner adjuster   20 Camshaft sprocket
21 Thrust plate   22 Jackshaft bearing   23 Jackshaft   24 Inlet valve   25 Valve seat (exhaust)   26 Exhaust valve
27 Valve seat (inlet)   28 Valve guide (inlet)   29 Spring seat (lower)   30 Valve spring (inner)   31 Valve spring (outer)
   32 Valve guide (exhaust)   33 Circlip   34 Camshaft (inlet valves)   35 Plug

Components of the valve gear

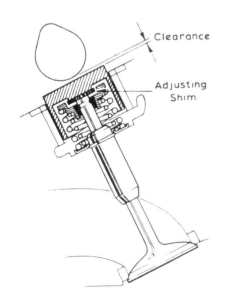

Valve clearance adjustment.

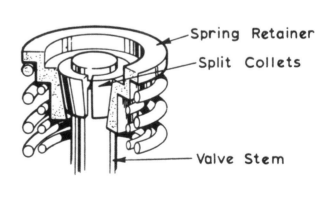

Valve spring retainer (upper spring seat)

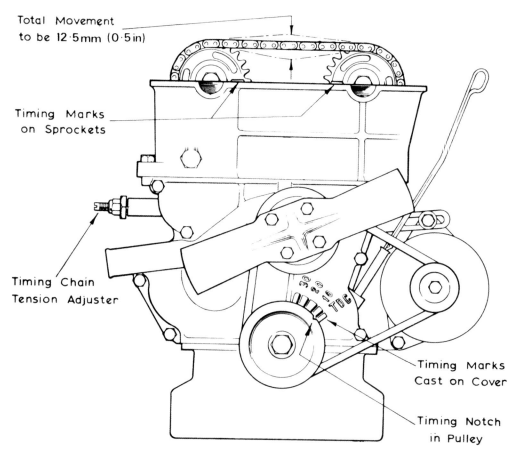

Timing marks

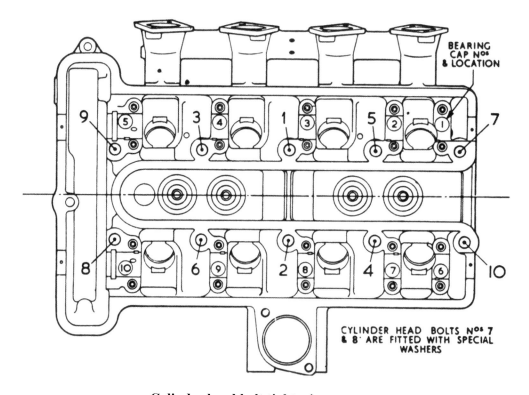

Cylinder head bolt tightening sequence

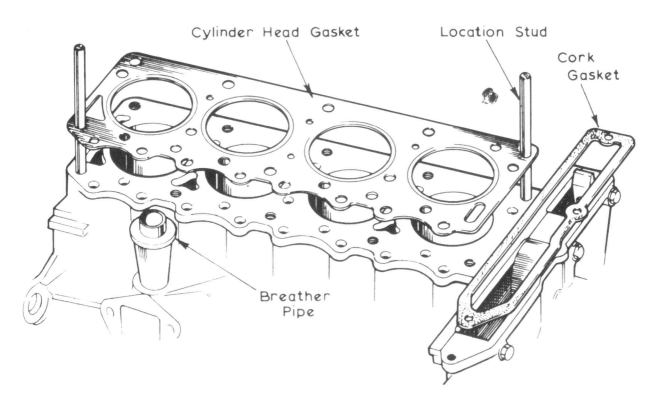

Cylinder head location studs and gaskets

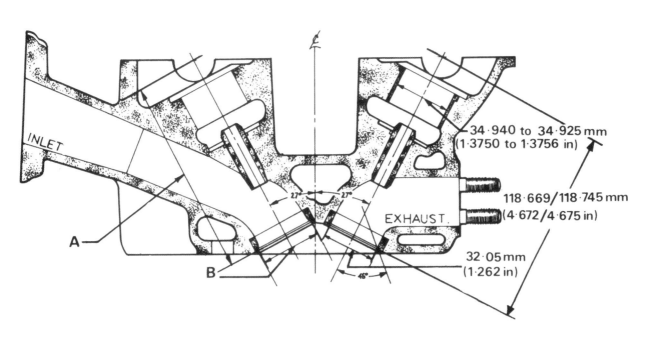

Key A 119.329/119.405mm (4.698/4.701in) or (big valve) 119.838/119.913mm (4.718/4.712in)
B 37.16mm (1.467in) or (big valve) 38.10mm (1.500in)

Valve seat measurements and angles.

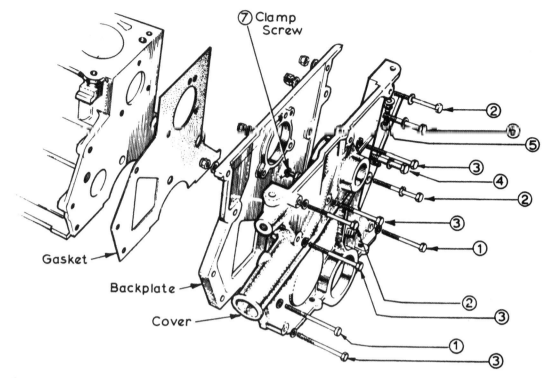

Key 1 Dowel bolts 0.25in UNC x 2.50in long   2 Bolt 0.25in UNF x 2.25in long   3 Bolt 0.25in UNC x 2.25in long
4 0.3125in UNC x 2.25in long   5 0.3125in UNC x 1.0in long   6 0.3125in UNF x 1.75in long   7 0.25in UNC x 0.75in long

Front cover mounting details

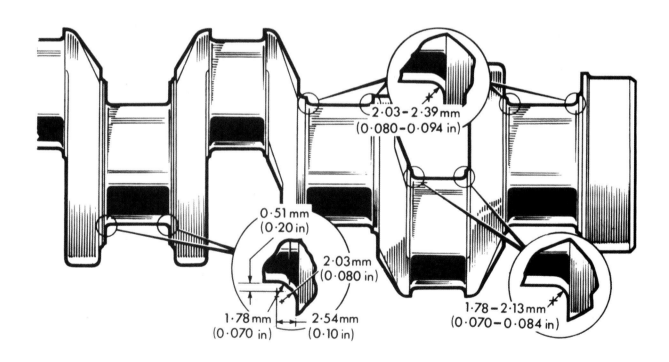

Crankshaft fillet radii

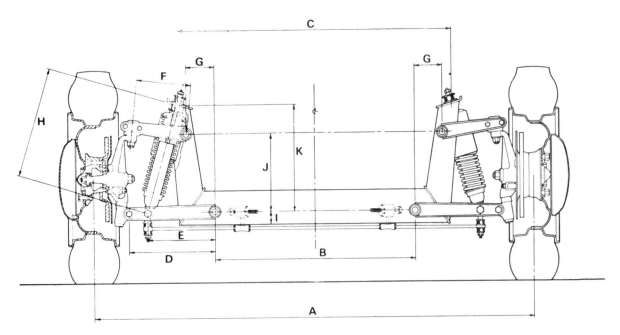

Front suspension, Elan and Elan +2 models. Dimensions are in millimetres (inches)

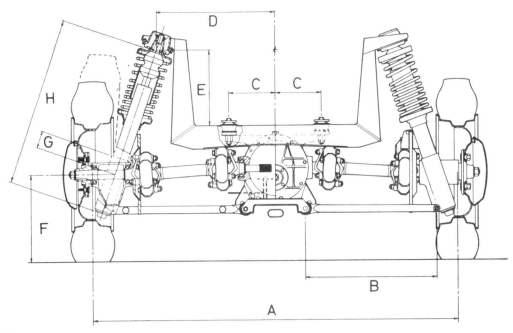

Rear suspension and final drive, Elan and Elan +2 models. Dimensions are in millimetres (inches)

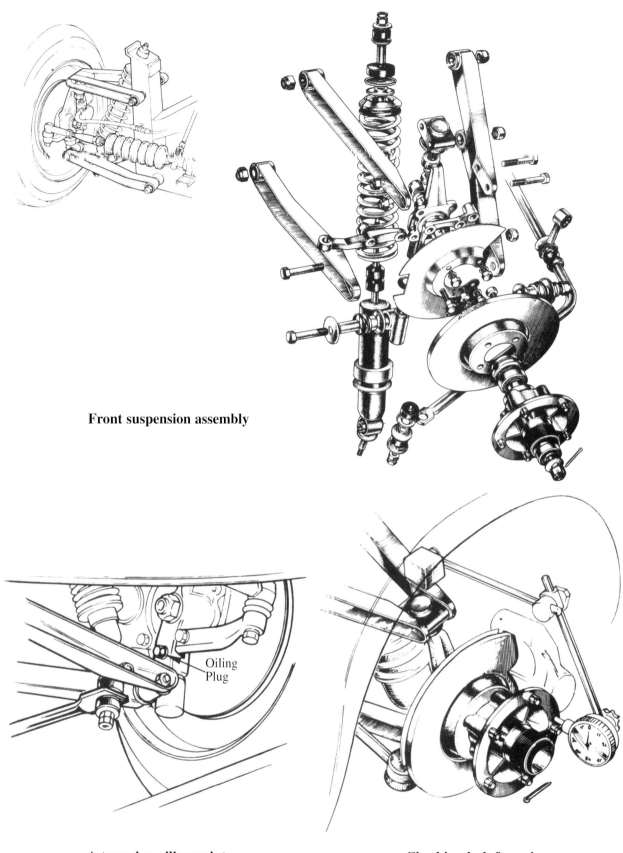

Front suspension assembly

Oiling
Plug

A trunnion oiling point

Checking hub free play

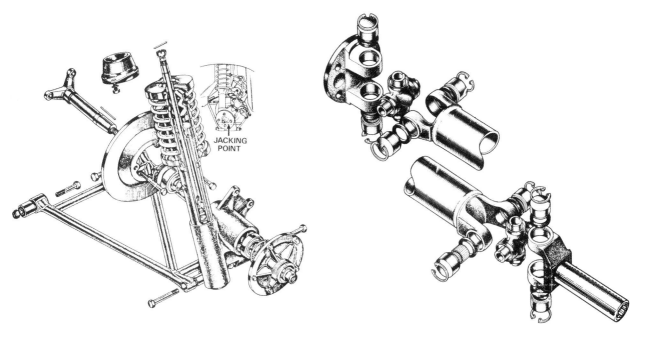

Rear suspension assembly

Propeller shaft universal joint assembly

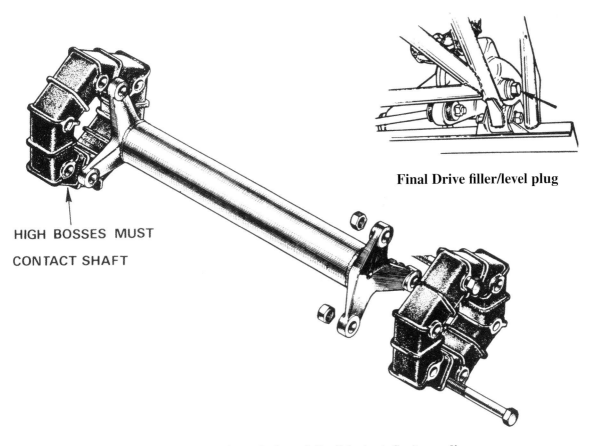

HIGH BOSSES MUST
CONTACT SHAFT

Final Drive filler/level plug

Intermediate shaft and flexible (rotoflex) couplings

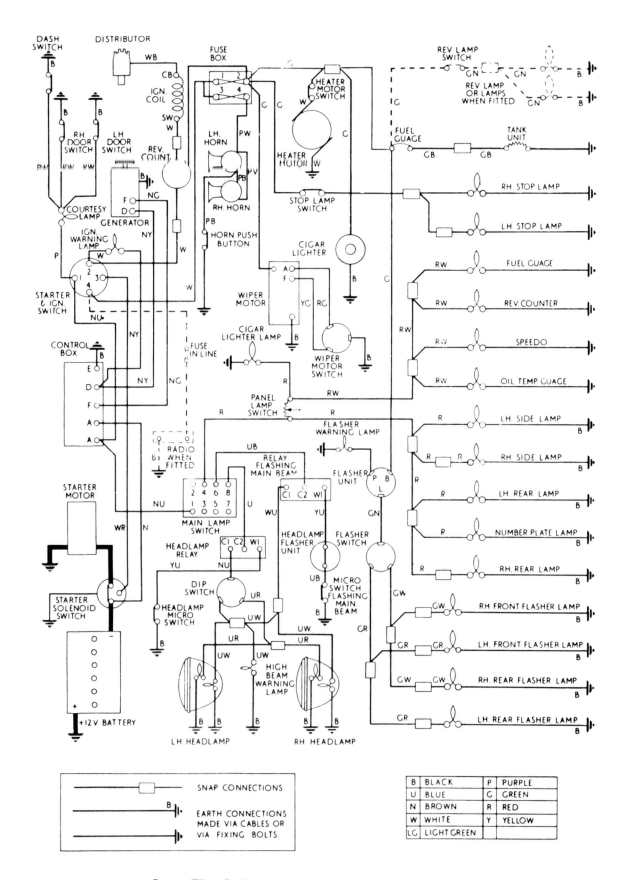

Lotus Elan Series 1 and 2, positive earth wiring diagram

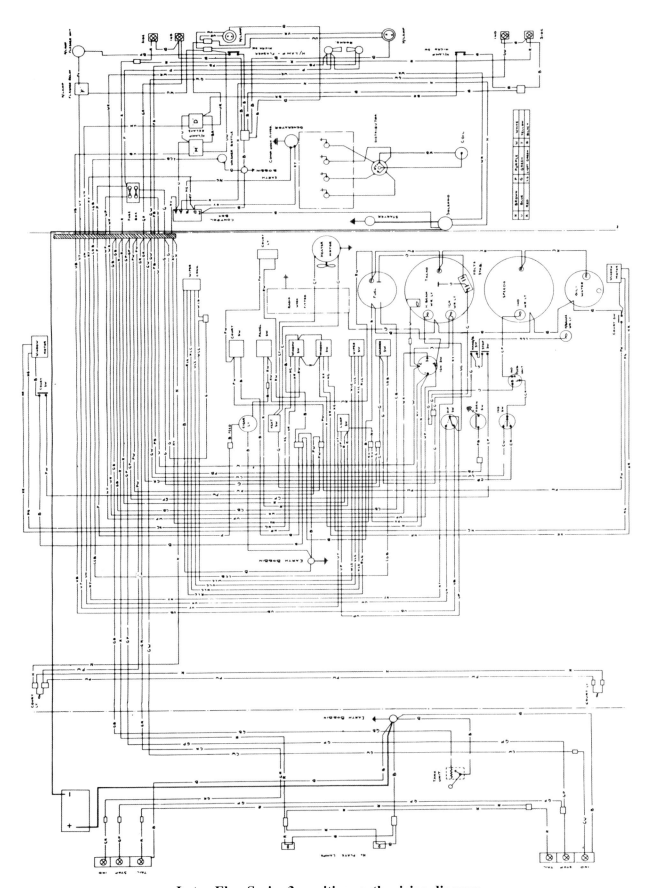

Lotus Elan Series 3, positive earth wiring diagram

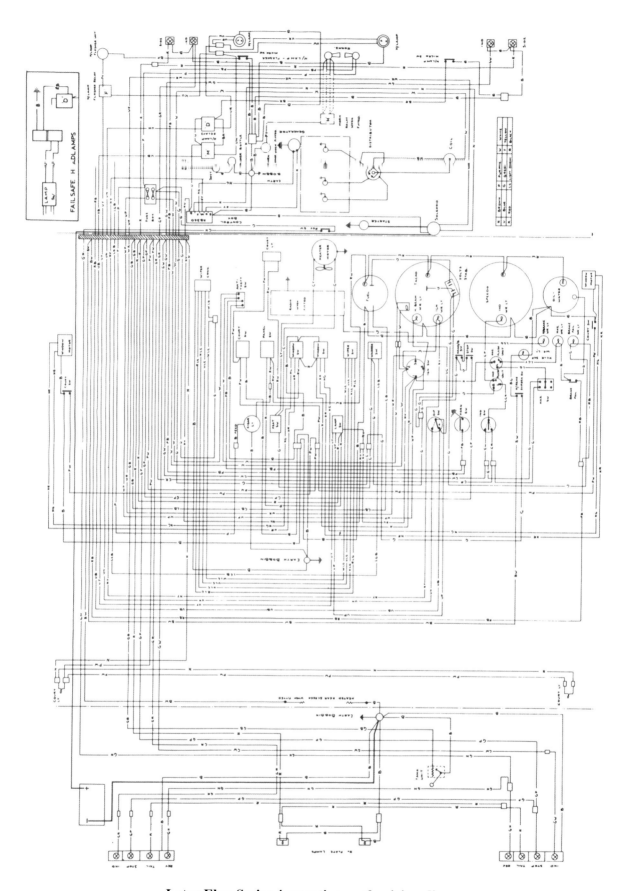

Lotus Elan Series 4, negative earth wiring diagram

TECHNICAL DATA

Dimensions are in millimetres (with inch equivlents in brackets) unless otherwise stated. If necessary, refer to Appendix v - Conversion Tables.

ENGINE

Engine type	4 cylinder, 4-stroke, water cooled
Engine capacity	1558cm^3 (95.06in^3)
Bore and stroke	82.550 x 72.746 (3.250 x 2.864)
Compression ratio :	
Elan	9.5 : 1
Elan Sprint	10.3 : 1
Elan +2	9.5 : 1
Elan +2 S130	10.3 : 1
Compression pressure	In excess of 11.03 bars (160lb in^2) at sea level
Variation (maximum)	1.38 bar (20lb in^2) cylinder to cylinder
Cylinder block	Cast iron
Bore :	
Grade 1	82.550 to 82.558 (3.2500 to 3.2503)
Grade 2	82.558 to 82.565 (3.2503 to 3.2506)
Grade 3	82.565 to 82.573 (3.2506 to 3.2509)
Grade 4	82.573 to 82.580 (3.2509 to 3.2512)
Cylinder head	Aluminium alloy
Depth :	
Small valve	117.8 to 117.9 (4.638 to 4.643)
Big valve	116.8 to 116.9 (4.598 to 4.603)
Minimum depth :	
Small valve	−1.14 (−0.045) below standard
Big valve	−0.254 (−0.010) below standard
Camshafts	Separate inlet and exhaust

Valve timing (degrees):

	Elan	Elan Sprint, S/E and Elan +2
Inlet opens BTDC	22	26
Inlet closes ABDC	62	66
Exhaust opens BBDC	62	66
Exhaust closes ATDC	22	26

End float	0.076 to 0.254 (0.003 to 0.010)
Journal diameters (5)	25.400 to 25.413 (1.0000 to 1.0005)
Running clearance	0.013 to 0.050 (0.0005 to 0.0020)
Cam followers :	
Bore in head	Refer to Manual
Follower diameter	34.904 to 34.912 (1.3742 to 1.3745)
Clearance with bore	0.013 to 0.036 (0.0005 to 0.0014)
Camshaft drive	Chain, tensioner and sprockets
Jackshaft	Driven by camshaft drive chain
End float	0.063 to 0.190 (0.0025 to 0.0075)
Journal diameters (3)	39.624 to 39.637 (1.5600 to 1.5605)
Running clearance	0.025 to 0.050 (0.001 to 0.002)
Crankshaft	Cast iron
Main journal diameters (5)	53.987 to 54.000 (2.1255 to 2.1260)
Crankpin diameters (4)	49.201 to 49.214 (1.9370 to 1.9375)
End float	0.076 to 0.203 (0.003 to 0.008)
Controlled by	Centre bearing thrust washers

Running clearance:
Main journals	0.038 to 0.076 (0.0015 to 0.0030)
Big-ends	0.013 to 0.051 (0.0005 to 0.0022)
Undersize on regrind	−0.762 (−0.030) on diameter (maximum)

Flywheel .. ..   Clutch operates on rear face
Face runout .. ..   0.101 (0.004) maximum
Ring gear runout:
Lateral	0.406 (0.016) maximum
Radial	0.152 (0.006) maximum

Connecting rods .. ..   Forged steel, H-section
End float on crankpin	0.101 to 0.254 (0.004 to 0.010)
Running clearance	0.013 to 0.0513 (0.0005 to 0.0022)
Small-end bore	Bushed
Grade A (silver)	20.635 to 20.637 (0.8124 to 0.8125)
Grade B (green)	20.637 to 20.642 (0.8125 to 0.8127)

Gudgeon pins .. ..   Floating, circlip located
Diameter:
Grade A	20.627 to 20.628 (0.8121 to 0.8122)
Grade B	20.628 to 20.632 (0.8122 to 0.8123)
Class of fit	Finger push-fit

Pistons .. ..   Tin plated aluminium alloy
Diameter, A type:
Grade 1	82.474 to 82.481 (3.2470 to 3.2473)
Grade 2	82.481 to 82.489 (3.2473 to 3.2476)
Grade 3	82.489 to 82.497 (3.2476 to 3.2479)
Grade 4	82.497 to 82.504 (3.2479 to 3.2482)

Diameter, C type:
Grade 1	82.466 to 82.474 (3.2467 to 3.2470)
Grade 2	82.474 to 82.481 (3.2470 to 3.2473)
Grade 3	82.481 to 82.489 (3.2473 to 3.2476)
Grade 4	82.489 to 82.497 (3.2476 to 3.2479)
Weight variation per set	4g maximum

Clearance in cylinder bore:
A type	0.068 to 0.083 (0.0027 to 0.0033)
C type	0.076 to 0.091 (0.0030 to 0.0036)
Gudgeon pin offset	1.016 (0.040) towards thrust face

Piston rings .. ..   Two compression, one oil control
Gap, fitted:
Compression rings	0.229 to 0.356 (0.009 to 0.014)
Oil control ring	0.254 to 0.508 (0.010 to 0.020)

Ring to groove clearance:
Compression rings	0.041 to 0.076 (0.0016 to 0.0030)
Oil control ring	0.046 to 0.097 (0.0018 to 0.0038)

Valves .. ..   Seat face angle, 45°
Clearance (cold):
Inlet	0.127 to 0.177 (0.005 to 0.007)
Exhaust (to engine No 9951)	0.152 to 0.203 (0.006 to 0.008)
Exhaust (from engine No 9952) ..	0.228 to 0.279 (0.009 to 0.011)

Head diameter:
Inlet (except Sprint and S 130) ..	38.760 to 38.862 (1.526 to 1.530)
Inlet (Sprint and S 130)	39.624 to 39.776 (1.560 to 1.566)
Exhaust	33.553 to 33.655 (1.321 to 1.325)

Stem diameter:
Inlet	7.874 to 7.899 (0.310 to 0.311)
Exhaust	7.874 to 7.899 (0.310 to 0.311)

Clearance in guide:		
Inlet	..	0.007 to 0.058 (0.0003 to 0.0023)
Exhaust ..	..	0.063 to 0.076 (0.0025 to 0.0030)

Valve springs .. .. .. Two per valve

Free length:
Inner	..	28.70 (1.130)
Outer ..	..	36.83 (1.450)

Valve guides:

Bore diameter (unreamed) .. 7.91 to 7.93 (0.3113 to 0.3123), ream to suit stem after fitting

Length .. .. 38.61 (1.520) inlet, 37.86 (1.480) exhaust

Fitted height above head .. 8.128 (0.320)

Lubrication .. .. .. Dual rotor pump, fullflow filter

Oil pressure (hot) .. .. 2.41 to 2.76 bar (35 to 40lb in^2)

Oil:
Temperate climates	..	SAE 20W/50 of reputable brand
Cold climates ..	..	SAE 10W/40 of reputable brand

FUEL SYSTEM

Pump, type .. .. .. Mechanical, actuated from the jackshaft

Pressure .. .. .. 0.086 to 0.172 bar (1.25 to 2.50lb in^2)

Air cleaner .. .. .. Dry paper element

Carburetters .. .. .. Two Weber, two Zenith-Stromberg or two Dellorto

Slow-running speed:

Weber .. .. .. 800 to 900r/min

Zenith-Stromberg:
Non-exhaust emission	..	800 to 900r/min
Exhaust emission	..	950r/min

Weber carburetters:

Elan models .. .. .. 40 DCOE 18

	Std	SE	
Choke ..	30mm	32mm	–
Main jet ..	115	115	–
Air correction jet ..	200	150	–
Slow-running jet ..	45 F9	50 F8	–
Accelerator pump jet ..	40	40	–

Elan models .. .. .. 40 DCOE 31

	Std	SE	Sprint, S130
Choke ..	30mm	32mm	33mm
Main jet ..	115	115	120
Air correction jet ..	200	150	155
Slow-running jet ..	50 F8	50 F8	50 F8
Accelerator pump jet ..	40	40	35

Elan +2 models .. .. 40 DCOE 31

Choke ..	30mm	32mm	33mm
Main jet ..	110	115	120
Air correction jet ..	155	150	155
Slow-running jet ..	45 F8	45 F8	50 F8
Accelerator pump jet ..	35	35	35

Elan and Elan +2 models:
Common settings ..	..	40 DCOE 18 and 40 DCOE 31
Accelerator pump stroke ..	..	10mm
Starter air jet ..	..	100
Starter petrol jet ..	..	F 5/100

Emulsion tube	F 11
Needle valve	1.75

Ait trumpet length:
40 DCOE 18 carburetters	44.4mm
40 DCOE 31 carburetters	38.0mm

Zenith-Stromberg carburetters:

Non-exhaust emission	175 CD 2S	–
Exhaust emission	–	175 CD 2SE
Needle	B 1Y	B 1G
Spring colour	Natural	Blue/black
Damper oil	SAE 20W/50	SAE 20W/50

Identification:
Front	Suffix S 710
Rear	Suffix S 711

Type:
E26	Fixed needle B 1G with idle return valve
G26	Fixed needle B 1G, throttle edge drillings, idle return valve deleted
I26	Adjustable needle B 1Y with side entry balance pipe
J26	Adjustable needle B 2AR with overhead balance pipe
F26	Fixed needle B 1Y with side entry balance pipe

Dellorto carburetters .. .. .. | Colour coded RED
Domestic	DHLA 40
European ECE 15	DHLA 40E

Identification:
Front	Suffix S 0710W
Rear	Suffix S 0711W

Type	Q026	R026
Choke	33mm	32mm
Auxiliary venturi	7848-1	7848-1
Main jet	120	120
Main air corrector	130	160
Idling jet	50.02	50L
Idling jet holder	7850-2(120)	7850-1(140)
Pump jet	45 or 35	33
Starter jet	70	70
Main emulsion tube	7772-5	7772-5
Starter emulsion tube	7482-1.28	7482-1.28
Needle valve	150.33	150.33
Float assembly	7298-01	7298-02
Air trumpet length	40mm	40mm

IGNITION SYSTEM

Type	Coil and distributor
Firing order	1, 3, 4, 2

Distributor:
Make	Lucas
Type	23D4 or 25D4 (exhaust emission)
Points gap	0.35 to 0.40 (0.014 to 0.016)
Cam dwell	60° ± 3°

Ignition timing:
Static timing data	Refer to Manual

Dynamic timing data .. .. Refer to Manual
Sparking plug types and gaps .. .. .. Refer to Manual

COOLING SYSTEM

Filler cap pressure rating :
    Elan models .. .. 0.69 bar (10lb in²)
    Elan +2 models .. .. 0.48 bar (7lb in²)
Antifreeze solution .. .. Refer to Manual
Thermostat opening temperatures :
    Temperate climates .. .. 78°C (173°F), standard fitment
    Tropical climates .. .. 71°C (160°F)
    Cold climates .. .. 88°C (190°F)

CLUTCH

Make and type .. .. Borg & Beck, diaphragm spring
Operation .. .. Hydraulic
Fluid .. .. As for braking system
Driven plate diameter :
    With 4-speed gearbox 203 (8.0)
    With 5-speed gearbox 215.9 (8.5)

TRANSMISSION

Gearbox type .. .. 4 or 5-speed and reverse
Gearchange .. .. Manual, synchromesh on all forward ratios

Gearbox ratios (: 1) :

	Semi-close	*Close*	*5-speed*
Reverse	3.324	2.807	3.467
1	2.972	2.510	3.200
2	2.009	1.636	2.010
3	1.396	1.230	1.370
4	1.000	1.000	1.000
5	N/A	N/A	0.800

Final drive ratio :
    Elan Series 1, 2 and early 3 .. .. 3.900 : 1
    Later Elan models .. .. .. 3.777 : 1
    Elan +2 models .. .. 3.777 : 1
    Optional .. .. 3.555 : 1
Lubrication :
    Gearbox .. .. EP80 gear oil of reputable brand
    Final drive .. .. EP90 gear oil of reputable brand

SUSPENSION

Type .. .. Independent, coil springs (front and rear
Geometry .. .. Refer to Manual

Springs :

Front :	*Elan*	*Elan +2*
Number of coils	19.6	15.6
Wire diameter	8.7 (0.342)	8.7 (0.342)
Free length	409 (16.08)	360 (14.19)
Fitted length	234 (9.22)	218 (8.60)
High free length	425 (16.75)	370 (14.59)
High fitted length	250 (9.86)	229 (9.00)

Rear:					Elan	Elan +2
Number of coils	..	..	..	..	8.7	9.7
Wire diameter	..	..	..	..	10.2 (0.40)	10.9 (0.43)
Free length	..	..	..	..	373 (14.71)	406 (16.0)
Fitted length	..	..	..	..	203 (8.00)	218 (8.60)

Hub bearing and float (front) .. .. .. 0.05 to 0.10 (0.002 to 0.004)
Toe-in (rear) .. .. Zero to 4.76 (0.1875)

Wheel camber:
Rear .. .. Zero to 1° negative
Front .. .. Elan 1 and 2, 0 to 0.5°; Elan 3 and +2,
0 to 1° positive

Wheel castor .. .. .. Early, 7°; later, 3° ± 5° positive
Kingpin inclination .. .. .. 9° ± 0.5°
Tyre pressures:
Front .. .. Refer to Manual.
Rear .. .. Refer to Manual.

STEERING

Type .. .. Rack and pinion
Toe-in (front) 4.76 (0.1875)
Turning circle diameter:
Elan Series 1, 2 and 3 .. .. .. 9.0m (29.5ft)
Elan Series 4 .. .. 10.0m (33.5ft)
Elan +2 .. .. 8.5m (28ft)

BRAKES

Make and type .. .. Girling hydraulic, disc front and rear
Hydraulic fluid .. .. Castrol/Girling Brake and Clutch
Universal fluid or DOT 3/4
Single/dual line .. .. Depending on model
Servo assistance .. .. Depending on model
Minimum pad thickness:
Elan 1.5 (0.06)
Elan +2 .. .. 2.5 (0.10)

Disc diameter:

					Rear	Front
Elan	..	..	..	..	254 (10.0)	231.8 (9.125)
Elan +2	..	..	..	..	254 (10.0)	254 (10.0)

Disc run out .. .. 0.10 (0.004) maximum
Handbrake .. .. Mechanical, rear wheels only

ELECTRICAL EQUIPMENT

Polarity of earth .. .. Depends upon model Refer to Manual
Fuses .. .. Two (12 on S models)
Battery .. .. 12-volt, Exide 6VTA 29L, 39amp/hr
Generator .. .. Lucas C40
Minimum brush length 6.0 (0.25)
Cuts in at .. .. 1450r/min and 13 volts
Maximum output .. .. 22amps at 2250r/min
Field resistance .. .. 6.0 ohms
Control box .. .. RB 106/2 or RB 340
Alternator: .. .. Lucas 17 ACR (12 pole, 3-phase)
Polarity .. .. Negative only
Minimum brush length .. .. .. 5.1 (0.20) free protrusion
Rectifier .. .. Integral diode
Maximum output (hot) .. .. .. 36amps at 6000r/min
Regulator .. .. Built-in
Regulator voltage .. .. 14.1 to 14.5
Rotor winding resistance .. .. .. 4.165 ± 5% ohms at 20°C
Stator winding resistance .. .. .. 0.133 ohms per phase

Starter motor	..	..	..	..	..	Lucas M 35G or 35J
Switching	..	..	..	..	..	Solenoid
Minimum brush length	..	..	..	..	8.0 (0.31)

CAPACITIES

				Litre	Imperial	USA
Engine (including oil filter)	..	..	..	4.25	7.5 pints	9.0 pints
Gearbox ..	..	..	..	1.00	1.75 pints	2.1 pints
Final drive ..	..	..	..	1.2	2.0 pints	2.4 pints
Coolant (with heater)	..	..	..	8.0	14.0 pints	16.8 pints
Fuel :						
Elan Series 1, 2 and 3 ..	..	..	..	45.0	10.0 gals	12.0 gals
Elan Series 4 ..	..	..	..	42.0	9.25 gals	11.0 gals
Elan +2 ..	..	..	..	59.0	13.0 gals	15.6 gals

DIMENSIONS

Track :						
Front	..	..	..	..	..	Refer to Manual
Rear	..	..	..	..	..	Refer to Manual
					Elan	Elan +2
Wheelbase	..	..	..	..	2134 (84)	2438 (96)
Ground clearance	..	..	..	152 (6)	165 (6.5)
Overall length	..	..	..	..	3683 (145)	4286 (168.75)
Overall width	..	..	..	..	1422 (56)	1682 (66.25)
Overall height	..	..	..	..	1150 (45.25)	1193 (47)

Appendix v

Conversion Tables

Inches	Decimals	Milli-metres	Inches to Millimetres — Inches	Inches to Millimetres — mm	Millimetres to Inches — mm	Millimetres to Inches — Inches
1/64	.015625	.3969	.001	.0254	.01	.00039
1/32	.03125	.7937	.002	.0508	.02	.00079
3/64	.046875	1.1906	.003	.0762	.03	.00118
1/16	.0625	1.5875	.004	.1016	.04	.00157
5/64	.078125	1.9844	.005	.1270	.05	.00197
3/32	.09375	2.3812	.006	.1524	.06	.00236
7/64	.109375	2.7781	.007	.1778	.07	.00276
1/8	.125	3.1750	.008	.2032	.08	.00315
9/64	.140625	3.5719	.009	.2286	.09	.00354
5/32	.15625	3.9687	.01	.254	.1	.00394
11/64	.171875	4.3656	.02	.508	.2	.00787
3/16	.1875	4.7625	.03	.762	.3	.01181
13/64	.203125	5.1594	.04	1.016	.4	.01575
7/32	.21875	5.5562	.05	1.270	.5	.01969
15/64	.234375	5.9531	.06	1.524	.6	.02362
1/4	.25	6.3500	.07	1.778	.7	.02756
17/64	.265625	6.7469	.08	2.032	.8	.03150
9/32	.28125	7.1437	.09	2.286	.9	.03543
19/64	.296875	7.5406	.1	2.54	1	.03937
5/16	.3125	7.9375	.2	5.08	2	.07874
21/64	.328125	8.3344	.3	7.62	3	.11811
11/32	.34375	8.7312	.4	10.16	4	.15748
23/64	.359375	9.1281	.5	12.70	5	.19685
3/8	.375	9.5250	.6	15.24	6	.23622
25/64	.390625	9.9219	.7	17.78	7	.27559
13/32	.40625	10.3187	.8	20.32	8	.31496
27/64	.421875	10.7156	.9	22.86	9	.35433
7/16	.4375	11.1125	1	25.4	10	.39370
29/64	.453125	11.5094	2	50.8	11	.43307
15/32	.46875	11.9062	3	76.2	12	.47244
31/64	.484375	12.3031	4	101.6	13	.51181
1/2	.5	12.7000	5	127.0	14	.55118
33/64	.515625	13.0969	6	152.4	15	.59055
17/32	.53125	13.4937	7	177.8	16	.62992
35/64	.546875	13.8906	8	203.2	17	.66929
9/16	.5625	14.2875	9	228.6	18	.70866
37/64	.578125	14.6844	10	254.0	19	.74803
19/32	.59375	15.0812	11	279.4	20	.78740
39/64	.609375	15.4781	12	304.8	21	.82677
5/8	.625	15.8750	13	330.2	22	.86614
41/64	.640625	16.2719	14	355.6	23	.90551
21/32	.65625	16.6687	15	381.0	24	.94488
43/64	.671875	17.0656	16	406.4	25	.98425
11/16	.6875	17.4625	17	431.8	26	1.02362
45/64	.703125	17.8594	18	457.2	27	1.06299
23/32	.71875	18.2562	19	482.6	28	1.10236
47/64	.734375	18.6531	20	508.0	29	1.14173
3/4	.75	19.0500	21	533.4	30	1.18110
49/64	.765625	19.4469	22	558.8	31	1.22047
25/32	.78125	19.8437	23	584.2	32	1.25984
51/64	.796875	20.2406	24	609.6	33	1.29921
13/16	.8125	20.6375	25	635.0	34	1.33858
53/64	.828125	21.0344	26	660.4	35	1.37795
27/32	.84375	21.4312	27	685.8	36	1.41732
55/64	.859375	21.8281	28	711.2	37	1.4567
7/8	.875	22.2250	29	736.6	38	1.4961
57/64	.890625	22.6219	30	762.0	39	1.5354
29/32	.90625	23.0187	31	787.4	40	1.5748
59/64	.921875	23.4156	32	812.8	41	1.6142
15/16	.9375	23.8125	33	838.2	42	1.6535
61/64	.953125	24.2094	34	863.6	43	1.6929
31/32	.96875	24.6062	35	889.0	44	1.7323
63/64	.984375	25.0031	36	914.4	45	1.7717

UNITS	Pints to Litres	Gallons to Litres	Litres to Pints	Litres to Gallons	Miles to Kilometres	Kilometres to Miles	lbs per in² to bars	Bars to lbs per in²
1	.57	4.55	1.76	.22	1.61	.62	.069	14.50
2	1.14	9.09	3.52	.44	3.22	1.24	.138	29.00
3	1.70	13.64	5.28	.66	4.83	1.86	.207	43.50
4	2.27	18.18	7.04	.88	6.44	2.49	.276	58.00
5	2.84	22.73	8.80	1.10	8.05	3.11	.345	72.50
6	3.41	27.28	10.56	1.32	9.66	3.73	.414	87.00
7	3.98	31.82	12.32	1.54	11.27	4.35	.483	101.50
8	4.55	36.37	14.08	1.76	12.88	4.97	.552	116.00
9		40.91	15.84	1.98	14.48	5.59	.621	130.50
10		45.46	17.60	2.20	16.09	6.21	.690	145.00
20				4.40	32.19	12.43	1.380	
30				6.60	48.28	18.64	2.070	
40				8.80	64.37	24.85	2.760	
50					80.47	31.07	3.450	
60					96.56	37.28		
70					112.65	43.50		
80					128.75	49.71		
90					144.84	55.92		
100					160.93	62.14		

UNITS	lbf ft to daNm	daNm to lbf ft	UNITS	lbf ft to daNm	daNm to lbf ft
1	.136	7.38	7	.949	51.63
2	.271	14.76	8	1.080	59.01
3	.406	22.13	9	1.220	66.38
4	.542	29.50	10	1.360	73.76
5	.678	36.88	20	2.720	147.52
6	.813	44.26	30	4.080	221.28

Appendix vi

CLASSIC LOTUS SPECIALISTS & CLUBS

The listing of specialist firms is for guidance only and does not constitute a recommendation.

My apologies to other firms and organisations I have not mentioned.

LOTUS SPECIALISTS

Christopher Neil Sports Cars
NORTHWICH
Tel 01606 41481

Paul Matty Sports Cars
BROMSGROVE
Tel 01527 835656

Classicar Automotive (Brake Specialists)
CHELFORD
Tel 01625 860910

Quorn Engine Developments (QED)
QUORN
Tel 01509 412317

Spyder Engineering
PETERBOROUGH
Tel 01733 203986

Mick Miller
SAXMUNDHAM
Tel 01728 603307

D J Dean
RUISLIP GARDENS
Tel 01895 674014

Chris Foulds
HUDDERSFIELD
Tel 01484 888552

SMS
SPALDING
Tel 01406 371504

Kent Sports Cars
CANTERBURY
Tel 01227 722000

BSS Parts
PRESTON
Tel 01772 601602

Banks Service Station
BANKS SOUTHPORT
Tel 01704 27959

GRP 2000
SOUTHPORT
Tel 0777 3206282

LOTUS CAR CLUBS

Club Lotus
41 Norwich Street
DEREHAM
NR19 1AD
Tel 01362 694459
Fax 01362 691144
e-mail clubhq@paston.co.uk

Lotus Drivers Club
PO Box 5548
Market Harborough
Leics
LE16 8ZD

INDEX

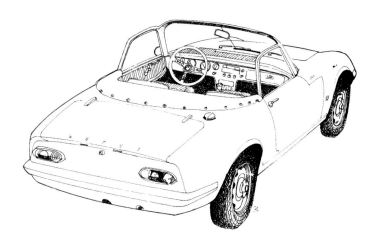

Further reading on the

LOTUS ELAN

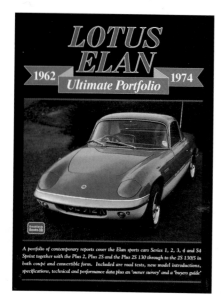

Lotus Elan Ultimate Portfolio 1962-1974

A portfolio of 62 contemporary Elan reports drawn from four continents. Covered are the Elan sports cars Series 1, 2, 3, 4 and S4 Sprint together with the Plus 2, Plus 2S and the Plus 2S 130 through to the 2S 130/5 in both coupé and convertible form. Included are road tests, new model introductions, specifications, technical and performance data plus an 'owner survey' and a 'buyers guide'. 216 pages with over 350 illustrations (some in colour). Soft bound.

Lotus Elan Owners Workshop Manual

Re-issue of Autobooks' highly respected workshop manual. Covering: Engine, fuel and cooling systems, ignition, clutch, transmission, suspension, steering, brakes, electrics (with wiring diagrams) and bodywork plus advice on maintenance and overhaul. Covers all Elan models 1962-1974 and has a new chapter on Elan history. 168 pages, with over 250 illustrations. Soft bound. (OWM 600).

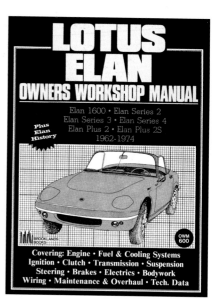

From specialist booksellers or, in case of difficulty, direct from the distributors:

Brooklands Books Ltd., P.O. Box 146, Cobham, Surrey, KT11 1LG, England Phone: 01932 865051
E-mail us at info@brooklands-books.com or visit our website www.brooklands-books.com
Brooklands Books Ltd., 1/81 Darley St., P.O. Box 199, Mona Vale, NSW 2103, Australia Phone: 2 9997 8428
CarTech, 11605 Kost Dam Road, North Branch, MN 55056, USA Phone: 800 551 4754 & 651 583 3471
Motorbooks International, P.O. Box 1, Osceola, Wisconsin 54020, USA Phone: 800 826 6600 & 715 294 3345

www.brooklands-books.com